DONLAD TRUMP AND THE MAGA MOVEMENT

Digby R. Kerr

Published by Digby R. Kerr, 2024.

DONLAD TRUMP AND THE MAGA MOVEMENT

First edition. September 3, 2024.

Copyright © 2024 Digby R. Kerr.

ISBN: 979-8227098054

Written by Digby R. Kerr.

Also by Digby R. Kerr

The Ripple Effect

The Ripple Effect: "A Fable About Embracing Change and Thriving in Uncertainty"

The Ripple Effect: "A Fable About Embracing Change and Thriving in Uncertainty"

Standalone

The Universal Code: Unlocking the Secrets of Happiness, Wealth, and Health

Mastering LinkedIn: A Comprehensive Guide to Building Your Profile, Growing Your Audience, and Leveraging Business Opportunities

The Universal Code: Unlocking the Secrets of Happiness, Wealth, and Health

Cross-Border Trade Compliance: Navigating the Global Marketplace

Report on Trends and Challenges in Logistics Hiring

"12 Steps to Success: Real-Life Stories of Manifestation and Transformation"

Psychological Warfare: 9/11 as a Tool for Manipulation and Control
DONLAD TRUMP AND THE MAGA MOVEMENT

Watch for more at https://www.linkedin.com/in/digbyrkerr/.

Table of Contents

Dedication

This book is dedicated to the millions of Americans who believe in the power of our great nation, to those who stand firm in their convictions, and to everyone who has ever dared to dream of a better, stronger America. To my family, friends, and all those who have supported me in this journey—your unwavering belief in the values of hard work, freedom, and prosperity fuels my passion to share these insights.

A special dedication goes to the men and women who have tirelessly worked to uphold the principles that make America exceptional. Your courage and perseverance in the face of adversity inspire us all.

And finally, to those who continue to fight for our nation's future—may this book serve as a testament to the strength of our collective resolve and a reminder that together, we can Keep America Great.

VOTE TRUMP NOVEMBER 5TH, 2024!

DONALD TRUMP
THE MAGA MOVEMENT
by Dight R. Kerr

Chapter 1: Introduction to Borderlines

Overview of Trump's Immigration Policies
The immigration policies implemented during Donald Trump's presidency have become a defining feature of his political legacy and continue to shape the discourse around his 2024 campaign. Central to these policies was a robust commitment to border security, which included the construction of a wall along the southern border and the deployment of additional resources to enforce immigration laws. This approach resonated with many Republican voters who prioritized national security and the belief that unchecked immigration posed a threat to American jobs and safety. Trump's rhetoric emphasized the need to reclaim control over the nation's borders, framing immigration as both an economic and cultural issue that required immediate attention.

In addition to physical barriers, Trump's administration pursued a series of regulatory changes aimed at limiting both legal and illegal immigration. These measures included the "zero tolerance" policy, which led to family separations at the border, as well as restrictions on asylum seekers and adjustments to visa programs. His administration's focus on merit-based immigration sought to attract skilled workers while reducing the influx of less skilled immigrants. These initiatives were positioned as necessary for enhancing economic growth and protecting American workers, appealing to a base that was increasingly concerned about job competition and wage stagnation.

The implications of Trump's immigration policies extend beyond immediate border security measures; they have significant ramifications for his 2024 presidential campaign. As he seeks to galvanize his supporters, immigration remains a pivotal issue that underscores his "Make America Great Again" slogan. Trump's ability to frame immigration as a central theme will likely influence voter mobilization strategies and grassroots campaigning efforts. By tapping into the sentiments of those who feel left behind by globalization and demographic changes, Trump's campaign is poised to use immigration as a rallying point to energize his base and attract undecided voters who prioritize border security.

Social media has played an instrumental role in shaping Trump's narrative around immigration. His adept use of platforms like Twitter and Facebook allowed him to communicate directly with supporters, bypassing traditional media filters. This strategy not only enabled him to disseminate his policies effectively but also to engage in real-time discussions with his base about the perceived threats of immigration. By framing opposition to his immigration stance as unpatriotic or dangerous, Trump has created a narrative that positions himself as a defender of American sovereignty, which resonates strongly with his supporters.

While Trump's immigration policies have garnered significant support from his base, they have also drawn considerable criticism from political opponents and various media outlets. Detractors argue that his approach has fostered a divisive atmosphere and undermined America's values of inclusivity and compassion. The ongoing debate surrounding immigration will likely continue to influence public perception and voter behavior as the 2024 election approaches. Understanding the complexities and ramifications of Trump's immigration policies will be essential for stakeholders across the political spectrum as they navigate the evolving landscape of American politics.

The Significance of Immigration in American Politics

The significance of immigration in American politics cannot be overstated, particularly in the context of the 2024 presidential campaign led by Donald Trump. Immigration has long been a pivotal issue that shapes political discourse, influencing voter sentiment and party platforms. For Trump, immigration is not merely a policy issue but a central tenet of his political identity, intricately tied to his vision of national sovereignty and economic prosperity. As his campaign unfolds, the implications of his immigration policies will resonate profoundly among Republican voters, framing the narrative of what it means to "Make America Great Again."

Historically, immigration has been a catalyst for economic growth in the United States, contributing to both labor supply and cultural diversity. However, the perception of immigration has shifted dramatically, particularly among conservative factions. Trump's rhetoric positions immigration as a threat to American jobs and security, appealing to the fears and frustrations of many working-class voters who feel left behind by globalization and demographic changes. This framing is not only instrumental in galvanizing support but also serves to delineate the Republican base, reinforcing a narrative of exclusion versus inclusion that is likely to dominate the campaign discourse.

The implications of Trump's immigration stance extend beyond mere rhetoric; they impact various voter demographics and economic proposals. His push for stringent border security measures and a re-evaluation of immigration pathways is designed to resonate with voters who prioritize job creation and economic stability. By emphasizing policies that prioritize American workers, Trump seeks to solidify his appeal among rural and suburban voters who may feel threatened by the prospect of increased competition for jobs. The intersection of immigration reform and economic policy thus becomes a crucial battleground in the 2024 election, influencing not only voter turnout but also the broader Republican platform.

Social media plays a pivotal role in how Trump disseminates his immigration policies and engages with his audience. His adept use of platforms like Twitter and Facebook allows him to bypass traditional media channels, directly addressing his supporters and shaping public perception. This strategy is particularly effective in mobilizing grassroots support, as it fosters a sense of community among voters who feel passionately about immigration issues. By framing immigration in a way that resonates with his base, Trump harnesses social media's power to amplify his message and galvanize action, essential components for a successful campaign.

As the 2024 election approaches, the significance of immigration in American politics remains a double-edged sword. While it serves as a rallying cry for Trump's supporters, it also invites scrutiny and criticism from opposition groups and the media. The discourse surrounding immigration will likely be contentious, with opponents highlighting the humanitarian implications and moral considerations of Trump's policies. Ultimately, the success of Trump's campaign will hinge on his ability to navigate this complex landscape, balancing the demands of his base with the broader implications of immigration on the American social fabric. The outcome of this electoral battle will not only define the future of Trump's political ambitions but will also shape the trajectory of American immigration policy for years to come.

Objectives of the Book

The primary objective of "Borderlines: Trump's Immigration Policies and the Future of America" is to provide a comprehensive analysis of the intersection between immigration policies and the broader socio-political landscape shaped by Donald Trump's administration. This book aims to dissect the implications of Trump's stance on immigration, particularly as they are poised to influence the 2024 presidential election. By addressing the nuances of his policies, we seek to engage Republican voters, government officials, students, and the general public in a meaningful dialogue about the future of America's immigration framework and its socio-economic ramifications.

Another vital objective is to analyze Trump's economic proposals, particularly those aimed at job creation, tax reforms, and trade agreements, and how these intersect with his immigration policies. The book will explore how the economic narrative is woven into the fabric of Trump's immigration stance, highlighting the perceived benefits and challenges that arise from his proposals. This analysis will not only inform readers about the economic implications of immigration reform but also position these policies within the larger context of Trump's vision for a prosperous America.

In addition to policy analysis, this book will delve into the role of social media in Trump's campaign strategy. Understanding how Trump leverages platforms like Twitter and Facebook to engage with voters is crucial for grasping his approach to grassroots campaigning. By examining his social media strategy, the book aims to shed light on how digital engagement has transformed political communication, particularly in mobilizing support for his candidacy among core voter demographics.

Furthermore, the book will assess the impact of endorsements and alliances on Trump's campaign. By investigating the relationships he has built with influential figures and organizations, we will uncover how these endorsements shape public perception and bolster his political capital. This exploration will also highlight the significance of grassroots movements and volunteer efforts, emphasizing their contribution to the overall momentum of Trump's 2024 campaign and the mobilization of his base.

Lastly, "Borderlines" will provide an evaluation of the opposition and criticism faced by Trump, especially as it pertains to his immigration policies. By contrasting his strategies with those of previous candidates, we aim to contextualize his approach within the broader historical narrative of American politics. This comprehensive examination will not only inform readers about the current political climate but also encourage critical thought regarding the implications of Trump's policies on various demographic groups, media portrayal, and public perception moving forward.

Chapter 2: Making America Great Again: Context and Implications

The Origins of Trump's 2024 Presidential Run

The origins of Donald Trump's 2024 presidential run can be traced back to the political landscape shaped by his previous administration and the subsequent events that galvanized his base. After leaving office in January 2021, Trump maintained a significant presence in American politics, positioning himself as the de facto leader of the Republican Party. His decision to run again in 2024 was influenced not only by a desire to reclaim the presidency but also by a belief that the policies he championed during his first term were essential to the nation's recovery from the challenges posed by the Biden administration. This narrative of return is deeply interwoven with themes of nationalism, economic revival, and a staunch defense of his immigration policies.

Central to Trump's 2024 campaign is his economic agenda, which seeks to resonate with voters who feel left behind by the current administration's policies. Analyzing Trump's proposals for job creation, tax reforms, and trade agreements reveals a strategy aimed at rekindling the economic optimism that characterized his first term. By promoting tax cuts and deregulation, Trump aims to appeal to both small business owners and the working-class voters who supported him in 2016. His campaign messaging emphasizes a return to "America First" principles, positioning himself as the candidate who can restore industrial jobs and revive the economy through strategic trade policies that prioritize American interests.

Immigration reform remains a cornerstone of Trump's platform as he embarks on his 2024 run. His stance on border security, characterized by promises to complete the border wall and enforce stricter immigration controls, continues to resonate with a significant segment of the electorate. The implications of his immigration policies are profound, as they not only reflect his commitment to law and order but also appeal to voters concerned about the economic impacts of immigration. By framing immigration as a critical issue affecting national security and job availability, Trump effectively mobilizes his base and draws contrasts with his opponents, who may advocate for more lenient policies.

Trump's mastery of social media as a campaigning tool cannot be overlooked. In the digital age, he has transformed how candidates interact with voters, utilizing platforms like Twitter and Facebook to disseminate his message directly to the public. This approach allows him to bypass traditional media channels, which he often criticizes as biased. His social media strategy encourages engagement and fosters a sense of community among supporters, reinforcing loyalty and enthusiasm for his candidacy. By effectively leveraging these platforms, Trump cultivates a grassroots movement that energizes volunteers and encourages voter mobilization, crucial components of his campaign strategy.

The 2024 presidential race is also shaped by the endorsements and alliances Trump forges along the way. Support from influential figures and organizations can significantly bolster a candidate's credibility and outreach efforts. As Trump garners endorsements from key Republican leaders and conservative organizations, he strengthens his position within the party and enhances his appeal to undecided voters. The interplay between his campaign tactics and the responses from political opponents and media outlets further shapes the narrative surrounding his candidacy. By analyzing these dynamics, one can better understand the multifaceted origins of Trump's 2024 presidential run and its implications for the future of America.

Key Themes in Trump's Campaign

Donald Trump's 2024 presidential campaign is characterized by a blend of familiar themes and new dynamics that reflect the evolving political landscape. Central to his platform is the rallying cry of "Making America Great Again," a slogan that not only encapsulates his vision for the nation but also seeks to galvanize a base that remains deeply invested in his leadership style and policies. This theme resonates strongly with voters who feel disillusioned by the current administration and nostalgic for what they perceive as a more prosperous and secure America. By framing his campaign around the idea of restoring national pride and economic vitality, Trump aims to connect with a broad spectrum of voters who prioritize stability and growth.

Economic policies and proposals are pivotal to Trump's campaign narrative. His strategies for job creation, tax reforms, and trade agreements are designed to appeal to both working-class Americans and business interests. By advocating for policies that prioritize American jobs and industries, Trump positions himself as a champion for economic nationalism. His proposals often include tax cuts for individuals and businesses, deregulation, and a focus on reshoring manufacturing jobs. This approach seeks not only to invigorate the economy but also to address the concerns of voters who have felt left behind in the wake of globalization and technological change.

Immigration reform is another cornerstone of Trump's campaign, reflecting his long-standing commitment to border security and strict immigration policies. His agenda includes enhancing border enforcement, reforming asylum processes, and emphasizing merit-based immigration. These policies are designed to resonate with voters who prioritize national security and are concerned about the implications of unchecked immigration. Trump's stance on immigration is likely to play a crucial role in shaping the 2024 election narrative, as it taps into broader themes of sovereignty and cultural identity that are significant to his base.

Social media strategy remains a powerful tool in Trump's campaign arsenal, allowing him to engage directly with voters and disseminate his message with unprecedented speed. By leveraging platforms like Twitter, Facebook, and Instagram, Trump not only communicates his policy positions but also frames the narrative around his candidacy. This approach enables him to bypass traditional media gatekeepers, fostering a sense of authenticity and direct connection with his supporters. Furthermore, Trump's adept use of social media has been instrumental in mobilizing grassroots campaigning, as volunteers and supporters organize efforts to amplify his message and reach wider audiences.

The influence of key endorsements and alliances is another theme that shapes Trump's campaign landscape. Support from influential figures and organizations can significantly bolster his credibility and mobilize additional voter support. Evaluating these endorsements reveals the strategic alliances Trump cultivates to enhance his appeal among various demographics. Additionally, voter mobilization techniques, including targeted outreach and engagement efforts, are designed to increase turnout among his base, particularly in crucial battleground states. Together, these themes not only articulate Trump's vision for America but also highlight the multifaceted strategies he employs as he seeks to reclaim the presidency in 2024.

The Appeal of "America First"

The "America First" mantra has become a cornerstone of Donald Trump's political identity, resonating deeply with a wide array of voters who feel overlooked by traditional political elites. This slogan encapsulates a broader message that emphasizes national sovereignty, economic independence, and the prioritization of American citizens in policy decisions. As Trump gears up for the 2024 presidential election, this appeal is likely to play a significant role in his campaign strategy, as it has in past elections. The appeal lies not only in its simplicity but also in its ability to invoke a sense of nationalism that many Americans find reassuring in a rapidly changing global landscape.

At the heart of the "America First" approach is a commitment to economic policies that are designed to benefit American workers. Trump's proposals for job creation, tax reforms, and trade agreements are framed as necessary measures to restore the economic might of the United States. By advocating for protectionist trade policies and a reduction in corporate taxes, Trump positions himself as a champion of the average American worker who has been adversely affected by globalization and foreign competition. This economic narrative resonates particularly well with blue-collar voters in rural areas, who feel that their needs have been neglected by previous administrations.

Immigration reform is another critical element of the "America First" platform, which emphasizes stringent border security measures and a reevaluation of the immigration system. Trump's rhetoric around immigration taps into fears regarding job competition and national security, framing the issue in a way that garners strong emotional responses from his base. The implications of this stance for the 2024 campaign are profound, as it mobilizes voters who prioritize border security and perceive immigration as a threat to their livelihoods and safety. By maintaining a tough stance on immigration, Trump seeks to reinforce his image as a leader who prioritizes the interests of American citizens.

In the digital age, Trump's mastery of social media has been pivotal in amplifying the "America First" message and engaging voters directly. His ability to bypass traditional media channels allows him to connect with his base in a manner that feels intimate and immediate. Through platforms like Twitter and Facebook, Trump disseminates his policies and ideas while simultaneously addressing criticisms and rallying support. This grassroots engagement strategy not only energizes existing supporters but also attracts undecided voters who may be swayed by his direct and often controversial communication style. The interplay between social media and the "America First" narrative creates a powerful tool for mobilization as the campaign progresses.

Lastly, the effectiveness of the "America First" appeal is further bolstered by key endorsements and alliances that lend credibility to Trump's campaign. Influential figures and organizations that align with his vision can significantly impact voter perceptions and turnout. By cultivating these relationships, Trump aims to solidify a coalition of support that spans various demographics, enhancing his electoral prospects. The combination of a focused message, targeted economic policies, and strategic grassroots campaigning positions the "America First" ideology as a formidable force in the upcoming election, ensuring that it remains a focal point in discussions about the future of America.

Chapter 3: Economic Policies and Proposals

Job Creation Strategies

Job creation strategies are at the forefront of economic discussions as the nation prepares for the 2024 presidential election. Under the banner of "Making America Great Again," Trump's approach to job creation hinges on a multifaceted strategy that combines tax reforms, trade agreements, and deregulation. These elements are designed to stimulate economic growth by encouraging investment and fostering an environment where businesses can thrive. The underlying philosophy is that a robust economy leads to job creation, which in turn supports a vibrant middle class and reduces dependency on government assistance.

A key component of Trump's job creation strategy is his proposed tax reforms, aimed at lowering corporate tax rates and simplifying the tax code. By reducing the tax burden on businesses, the argument posits that companies will have more capital to invest in expansion and hiring. This approach reflects a belief in supply-side economics, where lower taxes are seen as a catalyst for economic growth. Additionally, tax incentives for businesses that invest in underserved areas or create jobs in specific sectors could further enhance the effectiveness of these reforms, targeting job creation where it is needed most.

Trade agreements also play a crucial role in Trump's job creation strategy. The administration's focus on renegotiating existing agreements and establishing new ones seeks to prioritize American interests and protect domestic jobs. By advocating for fair trade practices, Trump emphasizes the importance of ensuring that American workers are not undercut by foreign competition. This strategy includes addressing issues related to tariffs and import quotas, which are designed to level the playing field for American manufacturers. Such policies resonate particularly with voters in key demographics who may feel threatened by globalization and its impact on local job markets.

Deregulation is another pillar of Trump's approach to job creation. The belief is that reducing regulatory burdens on businesses will empower them to hire more workers and innovate without the constraints of excessive government oversight. This strategy appeals to many in the Republican base who view regulations as impediments to growth. By advocating for a streamlined regulatory environment, Trump aims to create a climate that fosters entrepreneurial spirit and attracts new businesses to the American market, thereby generating employment opportunities.

As the 2024 campaign unfolds, these job creation strategies will be critical in shaping the narrative around Trump's economic policies. The effectiveness of these proposals will be scrutinized not only by political opponents but also by the media and the electorate. Voter mobilization techniques, including outreach efforts that emphasize the tangible benefits of these policies, will be essential in garnering support. By connecting job creation directly to the everyday lives of Americans, Trump's campaign can strengthen its appeal and potentially secure a path to victory in the upcoming election.

Tax Reform Proposals

Tax reform has been a central pillar of Donald Trump's economic agenda, and as he gears up for the 2024 presidential run, proposals for tax reform are likely to play a pivotal role in shaping his campaign narrative. Trump's previous administration made significant strides in altering the tax landscape, most notably through the Tax Cuts and Jobs Act of 2017, which aimed to reduce the corporate tax rate and provide tax relief for middle-class families. As he positions himself for another term, the focus on tax reform will likely include a combination of extending these past cuts and introducing new measures designed to spur economic growth, attract investment, and enhance job creation.

One of the key elements in Trump's tax reform proposals is the simplification of the tax code. The complexity of the current tax system has long been a point of contention among taxpayers and businesses alike. By advocating for a streamlined tax structure, Trump's campaign seeks to resonate with Americans who feel overwhelmed by the current regulations. Simplification can potentially lead to increased compliance and reduced administrative costs for businesses, thereby incentivizing expansion and hiring. This aligns with Trump's broader message of economic revitalization, emphasizing that a more accessible tax system can unlock opportunities for innovation and growth.

In addition to simplification, Trump's proposals may include targeted tax incentives aimed at specific sectors, such as renewable energy or technology. By promoting investments in these industries, the campaign can appeal to both traditional Republican values of free enterprise and the growing interest in sustainable practices among younger voters. This dual approach not only aims to stimulate immediate job creation but also addresses the long-term economic challenges posed by global competitiveness and environmental concerns. Such incentives can further solidify Trump's stance as a forward-thinking leader, capable of adapting to the evolving economic landscape.

As part of the 2024 campaign strategy, the narrative surrounding tax reform will also need to address the potential backlash from critics who argue that tax cuts disproportionately benefit the wealthy. Trump's approach will likely involve emphasizing the broader economic benefits of tax reform, such as increased wages and job creation. Engaging with grassroots movements will be essential, as grassroots supporters can serve as powerful advocates for tax reform within their communities. By effectively communicating the tangible benefits of his proposals, Trump can work to counteract negative perceptions and galvanize support from key demographics.

Ultimately, tax reform proposals will be a critical component of Trump's 2024 campaign, intertwining with his overarching themes of economic growth and job creation. As he navigates the complexities of the political landscape, the ability to articulate a clear and compelling vision for tax reform will be vital. By fostering an inclusive dialogue that addresses the concerns of various voter groups while promoting a robust economic agenda, Trump's campaign can position itself to reclaim the narrative around fiscal policy and its role in making America great again.

Trade Agreements and Their Economic Impact

Trade agreements serve as a critical pillar of the economic landscape, shaping the financial interactions between nations and influencing domestic job markets. In the context of Trump's vision for America, these agreements are not merely diplomatic tools but rather strategic instruments aimed at promoting American interests. As the 2024 presidential campaign unfolds, the impact of trade agreements on job creation, economic growth, and national security will be paramount. A comprehensive understanding of these agreements will illuminate their role in Trump's broader economic policies and how they resonate with voters seeking a return to prosperity.

Under Trump's administration, a shift occurred in how trade agreements were negotiated and implemented. The focus moved from multilateral agreements, which often diluted American influence, to bilateral negotiations that aimed to prioritize American workers and industries. This approach aligns with the "America First" doctrine, emphasizing the need to protect domestic jobs from foreign competition. The renegotiation of NAFTA into the USMCA exemplifies this strategy, aiming to bolster American manufacturing and agriculture while providing a framework that addresses modern economic challenges. Evaluating the outcomes of these changes will be crucial for understanding their effectiveness in revitalizing the American economy.

The economic impact of trade agreements extends beyond immediate job creation; they also influence consumer prices, innovation, and global competitiveness. Proponents argue that well-structured trade agreements can lead to lower prices and greater choice for consumers, as markets open up. Conversely, critics highlight the potential for job losses in specific sectors, particularly manufacturing, as companies may relocate operations abroad. The challenge lies in balancing these competing interests and ensuring that trade policies contribute positively to the overall economic ecosystem. As Trump positions his trade policies within the 2024 campaign, the narrative surrounding their impact on everyday Americans will play a pivotal role in shaping voter perceptions.

Furthermore, the implications of trade agreements are intertwined with immigration policies, particularly concerning labor markets. Many voters are concerned about the influx of foreign workers and its effect on domestic job availability. Trump's stance on immigration reform is closely linked to his trade policies, as he advocates for a comprehensive approach that not only secures the borders but also protects American jobs from being undercut by cheaper labor. This intersection of trade and immigration will be a critical topic during the campaign, as Trump seeks to reassure his base that he is committed to creating an environment where American workers can thrive.

In conclusion, trade agreements will be a significant aspect of the economic narrative in Trump's 2024 campaign. Analyzing their impact on job creation and economic stability will provide essential insights for voters and policymakers alike. As Republicans rally around Trump's candidacy, understanding the nuances of trade policy, its implications for immigration, and its effects on various demographics will be vital. The discourse on trade will not only shape economic policy but also influence the broader electoral landscape as America navigates its path toward renewed greatness.

Chapter 4: Immigration Reform

Trump's Stance on Border Security

Trump's stance on border security has been one of the cornerstones of his political identity and has significantly influenced his policies and proposals leading into the 2024 presidential campaign. Throughout his administration, he maintained a firm belief that strong border security is essential for national sovereignty, economic prosperity, and public safety. This perspective resonates with a substantial portion of the Republican base, who view immigration control as a critical issue affecting their communities and the nation as a whole. As the 2024 election approaches, Trump's immigration policies are expected to play a pivotal role in shaping his campaign narrative and voter mobilization strategies.

Central to Trump's border security agenda has been the construction of a physical barrier along the U.S.-Mexico border. He famously championed the slogan "Build the Wall," which encapsulated his commitment to preventing illegal immigration and drug trafficking. This initiative not only served as a rallying cry for his supporters but also positioned him as a decisive leader willing to confront what he termed a "crisis" at the border. Trump's approach emphasizes the need for enhanced security measures, including increased personnel for border enforcement and advanced surveillance technologies, which he argues are necessary to protect American jobs and communities from the economic impacts of illegal immigration.

In the context of economic policies, Trump's border security stance is closely tied to his broader agenda of job creation and tax reform. He argues that illegal immigration undermines wage growth for American workers, particularly in low-skilled labor markets. By advocating for stricter immigration controls, Trump positions himself as a defender of the American worker, appealing to voters who feel economically threatened by an influx of undocumented immigrants. This narrative not only reinforces his economic proposals but also galvanizes support among working-class voters who prioritize job security and economic stability.

Social media has become an essential tool for Trump to communicate his border security policies and engage with his base. Through platforms like Twitter and Facebook, he has the ability to bypass traditional media and deliver his message directly to voters. This strategy allows him to frame the narrative around border security in real-time, responding to criticisms and amplifying support among his followers. Trump's adept use of social media enables him to mobilize grassroots campaigns effectively, encouraging volunteer efforts and fostering a sense of urgency around the issue of border security as a defining feature of his 2024 candidacy.

Finally, the implications of Trump's border security policies extend beyond rhetoric; they shape his relationships with key endorsements and alliances within the Republican Party.

Influential figures and organizations that prioritize immigration control are likely to bolster Trump's campaign efforts, recognizing the electoral power of a unified stance on border security. As the 2024 election approaches, the interplay between Trump's immigration policies and his strategies for voter mobilization will be crucial in determining his success. By aligning his campaign with the values of his base and addressing their concerns about border security, Trump positions himself as a candidate who not only understands their fears but is also prepared to act decisively on their behalf.

Immigration Policies: Past and Present

The evolution of immigration policies in the United States has been a dynamic and often contentious journey, shaped by historical events, political ideologies, and public sentiment. From the early days of American history, where immigration was largely unregulated, to the more structured policies of the 20th century, the approach to border control and immigration has undergone significant changes. The past few decades have seen a polarizing debate on the effectiveness and morality of immigration laws, culminating in the Trump administration's controversial policies that have become a focal point in discussions surrounding the 2024 presidential campaign.

Under President Trump, immigration policy took a hardline stance, prioritizing border security and the enforcement of existing laws. The implementation of measures such as the "zero tolerance" policy, which led to family separations at the border, starkly illustrated the administration's commitment to a stringent approach. This not only stirred intense criticism from various advocacy groups but also galvanized a segment of the Republican base that viewed these policies as necessary for national security and economic stability. The framing of immigration as a critical issue resonated deeply with voters who felt that previous administrations had neglected the complexities of border control and its implications for American jobs and safety.

In contrast, the present landscape of immigration policy is characterized by a more nuanced debate, as the repercussions of Trump's policies continue to unfold. With growing concerns over labor shortages in key sectors of the economy, many are advocating for reforms that balance border security with the need for a flexible immigration system that accommodates skilled workers. The 2024 campaign is expected to reflect this tension, as candidates vie to articulate a vision that addresses both security and the economic contributions of immigrants. Trump's proposals will likely focus on streamlining processes for legal immigration while reinforcing stringent measures against illegal immigration, appealing to both traditional Republican values and the demands of an evolving economy.

Social media's role in shaping public perception of immigration policy cannot be overstated. Trump's adept use of platforms like Twitter and Facebook allowed him to bypass traditional media and engage directly with his supporters, disseminating his message on immigration effectively. This grassroots strategy has proven instrumental in mobilizing voters who may feel disenfranchised by the political establishment. As the 2024 election approaches, the focus will likely shift to how candidates utilize digital platforms to communicate their immigration policies and resonate with their base, particularly among younger voters who are becoming increasingly influential in the electoral process.

Ultimately, the ongoing debate over immigration policy will be a critical element of Trump's 2024 campaign. The historical context of immigration laws provides a backdrop against which current policies can be evaluated, and the impact of these policies on key demographics will be vital in shaping voter sentiment. As the electorate grapples with the complexities of immigration, candidates must strategically navigate this issue, balancing the demands for security with the economic realities of a diverse workforce. The outcome of these discussions will not only influence the trajectory of the 2024 campaign but will also have lasting implications for the future of America's immigration policies.

Implications for the 2024 Campaign

The 2024 presidential campaign is poised to be a defining moment for the Republican Party, with Donald Trump's immigration policies playing a pivotal role in shaping the narrative and strategies employed throughout the election cycle. As Trump seeks to reclaim the presidency, his approach to immigration will resonate deeply with his base while also posing challenges that could alienate moderate voters. The implications of this focus on immigration are multifaceted, affecting everything from grassroots campaigning to voter mobilization techniques. Understanding these dynamics is crucial for Republicans aiming to navigate the complexities of the electoral landscape in 2024.

At the heart of Trump's campaign is his commitment to border security and reforming immigration policies, which he has positioned as essential to national sovereignty and economic stability. His proposals, including building a wall and implementing stricter immigration enforcement, appeal directly to a significant portion of the Republican electorate that prioritizes these issues. However, this steadfast stance also raises the question of how it will impact broader voter demographics. While it energizes his core supporters, it risks alienating independents and moderates who may view such policies as extreme. The challenge for Trump's campaign will be to strike a balance between reinforcing his base and expanding his appeal to a broader audience.

Moreover, the economic implications of Trump's immigration policies cannot be overlooked. His plans for job creation, tax reforms, and trade agreements are intricately linked to his stance on immigration. Trump argues that a secure border will facilitate job growth by ensuring that American workers are prioritized in the labor market. Yet, critics contend that his approach may disrupt essential labor forces in industries reliant on immigrant workers. The campaign must address these economic concerns head-on, presenting a coherent narrative that connects immigration reform to overall economic prosperity, while also countering the criticisms from political opponents who may leverage these concerns against him.

Social media will undoubtedly play a crucial role in Trump's 2024 campaign strategy, particularly in how he communicates his immigration policies to voters. By harnessing platforms like Twitter and Facebook, Trump has the ability to bypass traditional media channels, directly engaging with his supporters and shaping the public conversation around immigration. This strategy not only allows for rapid dissemination of his message but also enables him to respond quickly to attacks and criticisms. However, the effectiveness of this approach will depend on the campaign's ability to resonate with voters beyond social media, ensuring that his policies are discussed in town halls, debates, and other public forums where diverse opinions can be heard.

Lastly, grassroots campaigning will be essential in mobilizing support for Trump's candidacy as he seeks to replicate the successes of his previous campaigns. Building a robust network of volunteers and local supporters will enhance voter outreach efforts, particularly in key battleground states. Endorsements from influential figures and organizations can further bolster this grassroots momentum, lending credibility to his immigration policies and reinforcing his position within the party. Ultimately, the implications of Trump's immigration stance for the 2024 campaign are profound, requiring a nuanced approach that addresses both the fervent support and the considerable opposition that his policies elicit. Navigating these complexities will be critical for the success of his campaign and the future direction of the Republican Party.

Chapter 5: Social Media Strategy

rump's Use of Social Media Platforms

In the realm of modern politics, few figures have harnessed the power of social media as effectively as Donald Trump. His adept use of various platforms has not only reshaped political communication but has also played a pivotal role in his electoral strategies, particularly as he gears up for the 2024 presidential campaign. Trump's social media presence allows him to engage directly with his base, bypassing traditional media filters that often convey a narrative unfavorable to him. This direct line of communication enables him to rally support, disseminate his policies, and react swiftly to events, making it a cornerstone of his campaign strategy.

Trump's approach to social media is characterized by a unique blend of personal branding and populist messaging. His tweets and posts often reflect his unfiltered thoughts, which resonate with many of his supporters who value authenticity over political correctness. This strategy not only solidifies loyalty among his base but also attracts undecided voters who may be disillusioned with conventional political discourse. By framing his messages in a way that speaks directly to the concerns of everyday Americans, Trump effectively creates a sense of community among his followers, positioning himself as a champion of the people against the established political order.

The implications of Trump's social media strategy extend beyond mere engagement; they also shape the discourse surrounding critical issues, including immigration reform and economic policies. Through targeted messaging, Trump can emphasize his administration's accomplishments, such as job creation and tax reforms, while simultaneously critiquing the policies of his opponents. This narrative control allows him to maintain a favorable perception among his supporters, making it easier to mobilize them for grassroots campaigning efforts, which are essential for voter turnout in the upcoming election. The ability to frame his policies in a relatable manner through social media enhances his appeal and reinforces his campaign's overarching themes.

Moreover, Trump's social media presence has proven instrumental in securing key endorsements and alliances, further bolstering his campaign's credibility and reach. Influential figures and organizations that align with his vision often utilize social media to publicly support him, amplifying his message and attracting additional followers. These endorsements are crucial not only for solidifying his base but also for appealing to broader demographics that might be influenced by the voices of respected leaders within their communities. As such, social media serves as a platform for creating a network of support that extends beyond traditional political boundaries.

In conclusion, Trump's utilization of social media platforms is a multifaceted strategy that significantly impacts his 2024 presidential run. It enhances voter engagement, shapes public discourse, facilitates grassroots efforts, and solidifies strategic alliances. As the campaign progresses, understanding the nuances of Trump's social media tactics will be essential for analyzing their effects on voter mobilization and the overall political landscape. The ability to navigate and leverage these platforms effectively may ultimately determine the success of his campaign and the future trajectory of American politics.

Engaging Voters Online

Engaging voters online has become a crucial strategy in contemporary political campaigns, particularly in the context of Donald Trump's 2024 presidential run. As the digital landscape continues to evolve, so too do the methods by which candidates connect with their constituents. For Republicans seeking to preserve and expand their voter base, understanding the dynamics of online engagement is imperative. This subchapter will explore how Trump's campaign leverages social media platforms, grassroots movements, and innovative voter mobilization techniques to strengthen his message and rally support.

Social media has emerged as a powerful tool for political communication, allowing candidates to reach millions with unprecedented speed and efficiency. Trump's adept use of platforms such as Twitter, Facebook, and Instagram has enabled him to disseminate his message directly to voters without the filter of traditional media. This direct engagement fosters a sense of community among supporters, who feel personally connected to the candidate. Furthermore, Trump's ability to generate viral content and stir conversations online plays a critical role in shaping public discourse, which is essential as he navigates the complexities of immigration reform and economic policy amidst a polarized electorate.

In addition to social media, grassroots campaigning remains a vital component of Trump's strategy. Mobilizing volunteers and local supporters creates an organic network of advocates who can amplify the campaign's message at the community level. Grassroots efforts not only enhance voter outreach but also empower individuals to take ownership of the campaign, fostering a sense of agency that resonates with the "Make America Great Again" ethos. By harnessing the enthusiasm of grassroots movements, Trump's campaign can effectively engage voters who may feel disenchanted with traditional political processes, thereby increasing overall voter turnout.

Voter mobilization techniques are also central to engaging the electorate in a meaningful way. Trump's campaign has utilized data analytics to identify key demographics and tailor messaging to resonate with specific voter groups, such as rural Americans or minority populations. These targeted strategies are designed to address the unique concerns and aspirations of various constituencies, making the campaign's policies on job creation, tax reform, and border security more relatable and impactful. By understanding and addressing the needs of these groups, the campaign can create a more inclusive narrative that encourages broader participation.

Finally, the interplay between media coverage and public perception cannot be understated in the context of Trump's 2024 run. The campaign must navigate opposition and criticism from political adversaries and mainstream media while simultaneously crafting a compelling narrative that highlights its accomplishments and future vision. Engaging voters online means not only promoting positive messaging but also effectively countering misinformation and negative portrayals. As Trump's campaign approaches the election, the ability to maintain a strong online presence will be critical in shaping voter attitudes and ultimately influencing electoral outcomes.

The Role of Social Media in Campaign Messaging

Social media has emerged as a pivotal force in modern political campaigns, serving as a direct conduit for candidates to communicate their messages and engage with voters. In the context of Donald Trump's 2024 presidential run, social media is not merely an adjunct to traditional campaigning; it is central to his strategy. The immediacy and reach of platforms such as Twitter, Facebook, and Instagram allow Trump to bypass conventional media gatekeepers, delivering his messages directly to millions of supporters. This direct line to the electorate empowers him to shape narratives, respond to criticism instantaneously, and rally his base around key issues, particularly those related to immigration and economic policy.

One of the most significant aspects of Trump's social media strategy is its role in reinforcing his brand identity. The slogan "Make America Great Again" resonates powerfully within his social media messaging, encapsulating his vision of a revitalized America. Through targeted posts, live streams, and engaging content, Trump effectively cultivates an image of strength and decisiveness, which appeals to voters seeking a leader who prioritizes national interests. This branding is particularly crucial in the context of his immigration policies, where he emphasizes border security and the need for reform. By consistently framing these issues through his social media channels, he not only keeps them at the forefront of public discourse but also solidifies support among his base.

Moreover, social media serves as a platform for grassroots mobilization, enabling supporters to organize and participate in campaign activities more efficiently. The ability to share content, rally supporters, and coordinate events allows for a grassroots network that is both dynamic and responsive. Trump's campaign has effectively harnessed this potential, utilizing social media to encourage volunteer efforts, disseminate campaign materials, and foster community engagement. This grassroots aspect is particularly important for increasing voter turnout, as it empowers supporters to take an active role in the campaign, thereby enhancing the sense of ownership and commitment to the cause.

The impact of social media on Trump's campaign extends beyond mere messaging; it shapes the overall narrative of his candidacy. Trump's adept use of social media enables him to counteract negative press and challenges from political opponents swiftly. By addressing controversies directly on his platforms, he can control the narrative and mitigate potential damage from critical coverage. This tactic not only resonates with his supporters, who often view mainstream media as biased, but also reinforces their loyalty and engagement. The interaction between Trump and his followers fosters a sense of community, making his campaign more resilient in the face of opposition.

In conclusion, the role of social media in Trump's 2024 campaign is multifaceted, influencing not only how he communicates his policies but also how those policies are perceived by the electorate. By leveraging social media effectively, Trump not only disseminates his messages on immigration and economic policies but also cultivates a robust grassroots movement that is essential for voter mobilization. As the campaign progresses, understanding the intricacies of this digital strategy will be vital for Republican supporters, policymakers, and political analysts alike, as it will significantly impact the dynamics of voter engagement and the overall electoral landscape.

Chapter 6: Grassroots Campaigning

The Importance of Grassroots Movements

The importance of grassroots movements in the context of Trump's 2024 presidential run cannot be overstated. As the political landscape continues to evolve, the power of ordinary citizens mobilizing at the local level has proven to be a vital force in shaping campaigns and influencing policy. Grassroots movements serve as a counterbalance to the institutional power of political elites, providing a platform for voices that might otherwise go unheard. In the case of Trump, these movements are not just supplementary; they are central to his strategy of appealing directly to the American people, leveraging their passions and concerns to drive his campaign forward.

Grassroots campaigning operates on the principle that engaged citizens can effect change from the bottom up. This approach fosters a sense of ownership among supporters who feel their contributions, whether through time, effort, or financial support, make a tangible difference. For Trump's 2024 campaign, harnessing grassroots enthusiasm is particularly crucial as he seeks to rally his base around his stances on immigration, economic policies, and national security. By tapping into the motivations of individuals and local organizations, Trump's campaign can cultivate a dedicated volunteer network that not only spreads his message but also mobilizes voters in key demographics that are essential for electoral success.

Moreover, grassroots movements often lead to a more authentic connection between candidates and constituents. For Trump, who has faced criticism from various quarters, the ability to engage with voters on a personal level through town halls, rallies, and community events enhances his relatability. This direct engagement allows for a more nuanced understanding of the specific concerns affecting different voter groups, particularly in areas heavily impacted by his immigration policies or economic reforms. The responsiveness of a grassroots campaign can help fine-tune messaging and strategies, ensuring that they resonate with the electorate's needs and aspirations.

In addition to enhancing candidate visibility, grassroots movements play a critical role in voter mobilization efforts. By organizing local events, door-to-door canvassing, and phone banking, these initiatives help overcome barriers to participation in the electoral process. As Trump's campaign gears up for 2024, effectively mobilizing his base—especially in swing states—will be paramount. Grassroots efforts can also counteract misinformation and provide reliable information about voting procedures, ensuring that supporters are equipped to cast their ballots.

Finally, the impact of grassroots movements extends beyond mere electoral mechanics; they shape the broader narrative of a campaign. In an era dominated by social media, the ability of grassroots supporters to share their experiences and perspectives amplifies the reach of Trump's message. The organic, grassroots-driven content resonates with many voters who may feel alienated by traditional media narratives. As such, the success of grassroots mobilization in support of Trump's candidacy reflects a shifting paradigm in political campaigning—one where the voices of the people are not just heard, but are instrumental in defining the trajectory of American politics.

Volunteer Efforts and Community Engagement

In the context of Trump's 2024 presidential run, volunteer efforts and community engagement play a pivotal role in mobilizing grassroots support. The success of any political campaign is often contingent upon the energy and dedication of its volunteers, who serve as the backbone of outreach initiatives. For Trump's campaign, this means harnessing the enthusiasm of supporters who are passionate about his immigration policies, economic reform proposals, and the broader vision of revitalizing America. By fostering a sense of community among volunteers, the campaign can create a network of advocates who actively promote Trump's message within their neighborhoods, thereby enhancing the overall voter mobilization strategy.

The Trump campaign has strategically focused on community engagement to cultivate a robust grassroots movement. This involves organizing town halls, rallies, and local events where supporters can gather, share their experiences, and discuss the implications of Trump's policies. These gatherings not only allow volunteers to connect with one another but also provide a platform for potential voters to hear directly from the campaign. By emphasizing personal stories and local concerns, the campaign can effectively resonate with the electorate, particularly within communities that feel overlooked by traditional political discourse. This grassroots approach is instrumental in building a narrative that aligns Trump's policy proposals with the everyday lives of Americans.

Social media also plays a critical role in enhancing volunteer efforts and community engagement. The Trump campaign has adeptly utilized various platforms to disseminate information, rally support, and encourage volunteers to take action. Through targeted messaging and engaging content, the campaign can reach a wider audience, galvanizing individuals who may not have previously participated in political activities. The immediacy and interactivity of social media allow for real-time communication, enabling volunteers to share updates, organize local initiatives, and mobilize their networks for events. This strategy not only amplifies the campaign's reach but also fosters a sense of belonging among supporters, reinforcing their commitment to Trump's vision.

Moreover, endorsements from influential figures and organizations can significantly bolster volunteer efforts and community engagement. When prominent individuals publicly support Trump's candidacy, it not only lends credibility to the campaign but also inspires volunteers to rally around a shared cause. These endorsements can serve as a catalyst for increased participation, as supporters feel empowered by the recognition of their values and beliefs by respected leaders. As volunteers engage with these endorsements, they can leverage them in their outreach efforts, creating a narrative that underscores the collective urgency of supporting Trump's policies, particularly in the realms of immigration reform and economic revitalization.

As the 2024 campaign unfolds, the effectiveness of volunteer efforts and community engagement will be closely scrutinized. The ability to mobilize supporters and translate enthusiasm into tangible voter turnout will be critical in determining the campaign's success. By fostering an inclusive environment that encourages participation, the Trump campaign can harness the collective power of its grassroots supporters, ensuring that their voices are heard. In doing so, they not only strengthen their electoral chances but also contribute to a broader movement aimed at reshaping the narrative surrounding America's future, reflecting a commitment to making America great again through active civic participation.

Case Studies of Successful Grassroots Initiatives

Case studies of successful grassroots initiatives reveal the power and potential of local movements to effect change, particularly in the context of political campaigns. As the 2024 presidential election looms, the role of grassroots efforts in supporting candidates like Donald Trump becomes increasingly significant. These initiatives often emerge from a deep-seated desire for change among constituents and reflect the values and priorities of the communities involved. Understanding these grassroots successes provides insight into how movements can mobilize support, engage voters, and ultimately influence policy agendas.

One notable example of a successful grassroots initiative is the Tea Party movement, which gained momentum in the late 2000s. This movement was characterized by its emphasis on limited government, fiscal conservatism, and a strict interpretation of the Constitution. The Tea Party effectively harnessed social media and local organizing to galvanize support, ultimately influencing Republican primaries and the broader political landscape. The movement's ability to connect with voters through town hall meetings, rallies, and online platforms underscores the importance of direct engagement in mobilizing political support. As Trump's 2024 campaign gears up, drawing lessons from the Tea Party's approach could be instrumental in energizing his base and expanding outreach.

Another compelling case study is the grassroots organizing seen during the 2016 election cycle, when Trump's campaign tapped into the frustrations of working-class Americans who felt left behind by traditional political elites. Local volunteer groups sprang up across the country, facilitating door-to-door canvassing and community events that fostered personal connections between voters and the campaign. This approach not only built enthusiasm but also cultivated a sense of ownership among supporters, making them feel integral to the campaign's success. As Trump's team looks to replicate this model for 2024, leveraging grassroots efforts will be crucial in maintaining momentum and ensuring voter turnout.

The role of social media in these grassroots initiatives cannot be overstated. Platforms like Facebook and Twitter have become essential tools for mobilization and communication, allowing campaigns to disseminate messages quickly and interactively. For instance, the #MAGA movement utilized these platforms to build a community of supporters who shared their experiences, concerns, and aspirations. This digital engagement, combined with face-to-face interactions, created a multifaceted approach to voter outreach that proved effective in galvanizing support. As Trump's campaign strategizes for 2024, an integrated social media strategy will be vital in reaching younger voters and those who primarily consume news online.

Finally, the importance of endorsements and alliances forged at the grassroots level cannot be overlooked. Local leaders and influential figures often serve as key conduits for rallying support, particularly in regions where Trump's policies resonate strongly. By building coalitions with community organizations, trade groups, and influential local figures, Trump's campaign can enhance its credibility and expand its reach. These grassroots alliances not only amplify the campaign's message but also foster a sense of unity among supporters, making it easier to mobilize voters in critical swing states. As demonstrated in previous elections, such strategic partnerships can significantly impact voter turnout and the overall success of a campaign.

In conclusion, examining these case studies of successful grassroots initiatives offers valuable insights into the strategies that can be employed in Trump's 2024 campaign. By harnessing the power of local movements, leveraging social media, and cultivating strategic alliances, the campaign can effectively engage voters and enhance its chances of success. As the political landscape continues to evolve, the lessons learned from these grassroots efforts will be crucial in shaping the future direction of American politics.

Chapter 7: Key Endorsements and Alliances

The Impact of Influential Endorsements

The landscape of American politics has long been shaped by the power of endorsements, especially when it comes to presidential campaigns. In the context of Donald Trump's 2024 run, influential endorsements play a critical role in solidifying his base and expanding his appeal to undecided voters. These endorsements not only lend credibility to his candidacy but also amplify his message, creating a ripple effect that can enhance voter mobilization efforts. As Trump navigates the complexities of immigration reform, economic policies, and social media strategy, the backing of key figures and organizations can significantly influence public perception and voter behavior.

Endorsements serve as a strategic tool for candidates, providing a form of validation that can resonate with specific demographics. For Trump, securing endorsements from prominent Republican figures and grassroots leaders can galvanize support among traditional conservatives while simultaneously attracting new voters who may be swayed by the credibility of the endorser. In a political environment marked by polarization, endorsements from respected individuals or organizations can bridge divides and foster a sense of unity among various factions within the Republican base. This is particularly important for Trump, as he seeks to consolidate support as he faces opposition both from within the party and from Democratic challengers.

Moreover, the impact of endorsements extends beyond mere rhetoric; they can also influence funding and resources available for campaigning. Notable endorsements often come with financial support or access to networks that can mobilize volunteers and resources for grassroots efforts. For Trump's campaign, aligning with influential figures can enhance his visibility and strengthen his grassroots initiatives, ultimately leading to increased voter turnout. This aspect is crucial as the 2024 election approaches, where the ability to engage and mobilize supporters will be pivotal in a closely contested race.

As Trump leverages social media to disseminate his message, endorsements can serve as powerful content for his online platforms. The endorsements not only provide material for campaign messaging but also create opportunities for engaging with followers. By highlighting endorsements on social media, Trump can amplify the voices of those who support him while also encouraging discussions among his base. This interplay between endorsements and social media strategy is particularly relevant in an era where digital engagement can significantly sway public opinion and enhance voter turnout.

In conclusion, the impact of influential endorsements on Trump's 2024 presidential run cannot be understated. They not only enhance his credibility and unify his base but also provide critical resources for effective campaigning. As Trump continues to navigate the multifaceted challenges of immigration reform, economic policies, and voter mobilization, the strategic use of endorsements will play a vital role in shaping the trajectory of his campaign. Understanding this dynamic is essential for Republicans, government officials, students, and all engaged citizens as they contemplate the implications of endorsements in the broader context of American democracy and electoral politics.

Assessing Alliances with Organizations

Assessing alliances with organizations is a crucial component of any political campaign, particularly in the context of Donald Trump's 2024 presidential run. For Republicans and supporters of Trump's agenda, understanding how strategic partnerships can bolster campaign efforts is essential. These alliances can take various forms, from endorsements by influential figures to collaborations with grassroots organizations that mobilize voters. Each partnership has the potential to enhance the campaign's visibility and credibility, thereby maximizing its reach and impact.

In Trump's previous campaigns, certain endorsements have proven pivotal. High-profile figures, whether they come from business, entertainment, or politics, can lend significant weight to a candidate's message. As Trump navigates his 2024 campaign, he will likely seek endorsements from key organizations that align with his economic policies and immigration reforms. These endorsements can serve to legitimize his proposals and resonate with specific voter demographics, reinforcing his position as a champion for their interests. The role of these organizations in shaping public perception and voter motivation cannot be overstated.

Moreover, grassroots campaigning remains a cornerstone of Trump's strategy. By aligning with local and state organizations, the Trump campaign can tap into existing networks of volunteers and activists who are already passionate about his policies. These alliances not only facilitate on-the-ground voter outreach but also create opportunities for supporters to engage directly with potential voters through events, rallies, and community initiatives. The synergy between the campaign and grassroots organizations can amplify messaging and mobilize a dedicated base, which is crucial for achieving high voter turnout.

In addition to grassroots support, the role of social media cannot be overlooked. Trump's adept use of platforms like Twitter, Facebook, and Instagram allows for real-time engagement and direct communication with constituents. Strategic partnerships with digital marketing organizations can enhance this effort, optimizing outreach strategies and targeting key demographics. By leveraging these alliances, the campaign can disseminate its message more effectively, countering opposition narratives and galvanizing support among undecided voters.

Finally, assessing the impact of these alliances requires a nuanced understanding of the political landscape. As Trump faces opposition from both political adversaries and media critiques, the effectiveness of his partnerships will be tested. The ability to navigate these challenges while maintaining strong alliances will be fundamental to his campaign's success. By strategically assessing and cultivating relationships with influential organizations, Trump can solidify his position as a leader who is not only attuned to the needs of his base but also capable of uniting various factions within the Republican Party to achieve a common goal: making America great again.

The Role of Political Networks in Campaigning

Political networks play a pivotal role in shaping the landscape of political campaigning, particularly in the context of Donald Trump's 2024 presidential run. These networks comprise a complex web of relationships among politicians, influencers, grassroots activists, and voters. They serve as conduits for information, resources, and support, amplifying the messages and strategies that candidates deploy. In the case of Trump, these networks are crucial for mobilizing his base, coordinating efforts, and maximizing outreach, which is especially vital in an election cycle characterized by heightened competition and polarized opinions.

One of the defining features of Trump's political network is its grassroots foundation. Grassroots campaigning has become increasingly significant, as it empowers ordinary citizens to engage actively in the political process. Through local events, door-to-door canvassing, and community outreach, supporters can communicate Trump's economic policies, immigration reform proposals, and social media strategies directly to their neighbors. This localized engagement not only fosters a sense of community but also reinforces loyalty among supporters, as they feel personally invested in the campaign's success. By harnessing the energy of grassroots movements, Trump's campaign can effectively penetrate various demographics, reinforcing his message of making America great again.

In addition to grassroots efforts, key endorsements and alliances significantly bolster Trump's political network. Influential figures and organizations lend their credibility and resources to the campaign, creating a ripple effect that can enhance visibility and appeal. These endorsements serve as powerful signals to voters, often swaying undecided individuals and solidifying support among established bases. Understanding the dynamics of these alliances allows the campaign to strategically cultivate relationships that align with its goals, facilitating a broader coalition that can rally around shared values and objectives.

Moreover, the utilization of social media platforms has transformed the nature of political campaigning, providing a direct line of communication between Trump and his supporters. This strategy allows for real-time engagement, enabling the campaign to disseminate key messages swiftly and counter opposition narratives effectively. Social media amplifies the campaign's reach, creating a virtual network that transcends geographic limitations. By leveraging these platforms, Trump's campaign not only engages existing supporters but also attracts new voters who resonate with his policies and proposals, particularly those related to economic growth and immigration reform.

Finally, the role of political networks extends beyond mobilization; they also serve as a crucial feedback mechanism. The interactions within these networks provide valuable insights into voter sentiment and concerns, informing the campaign's strategies and policy positions. By actively listening to constituents and responding to their needs, Trump can adapt his messaging and proposals to align with the priorities of key demographics, thereby enhancing his appeal. In this polarized political environment, understanding the dynamics of political networks is essential for any campaign aiming to achieve success, as they are integral to the interconnected nature of modern political engagement.

Chapter 8: Voter Mobilization Techniques

Strategies for Increasing Voter Turnout

Strategies for increasing voter turnout are critical for any political campaign, especially for one as consequential as Donald Trump's 2024 presidential run. To secure a robust electoral performance, it is essential to engage and mobilize the base effectively. The strategies must be multifaceted, addressing the unique concerns and motivations of various voter demographics while leveraging the strengths of grassroots campaigning, social media engagement, and targeted outreach initiatives.

First and foremost, understanding the demographic landscape is vital. Trump's base includes a diverse array of voters, from rural Americans to working-class individuals who feel left behind by traditional political establishments. Tailoring messages that resonate with these groups can significantly enhance turnout. This requires not only a clear articulation of Trump's economic policies, which focus on job creation and tax reforms, but also a connection to the emotional and social issues that matter most to these voters.

Campaign messaging should reflect an understanding of their daily challenges and aspirations, making the case that a Trump presidency is synonymous with their personal and community success.

Grassroots campaigning represents another crucial component of increasing voter turnout. Building a network of local volunteers can create a powerful ground game, fostering personal connections that resonate more than traditional advertising. By empowering supporters to take ownership of the campaign in their communities, the campaign can amplify its reach and encourage a sense of collective responsibility among voters. Organizing community events, town halls, and rallies can serve as platforms for direct engagement, allowing voters to voice their concerns while also reinforcing their commitment to the campaign.

In the digital era, social media plays a pivotal role in mobilizing voters. Trump's adept use of platforms like Twitter and Facebook allows for real-time engagement, enabling the campaign to disseminate its message quickly and effectively. Strategies should include targeted advertisements that speak directly to specific voter demographics, as well as interactive content that encourages sharing and discussion. Additionally, utilizing social media influencers who align with Trump's values can help broaden the campaign's reach to younger voters who may not be as engaged through traditional means. The key is to create a digital narrative that not only informs but also inspires action.

Furthermore, effective voter mobilization techniques must include a robust outreach program that addresses barriers to voting. This includes providing information on registration deadlines, polling locations, and voting methods, particularly for those who may face logistical challenges, such as rural voters. Developing partnerships with local organizations can enhance these efforts, ensuring that information reaches all corners of the community. Moreover, implementing get-out-the-vote initiatives, including reminders and transportation assistance, can significantly increase participation rates on Election Day.

Lastly, strategic alliances and endorsements can lend credibility and momentum to the campaign. Aligning with influential figures and organizations that resonate with the target demographic can enhance the campaign's visibility and appeal. These alliances can also facilitate access to resources and networks that are essential for mobilizing voters. By combining these strategies—understanding demographic needs, leveraging grassroots efforts, utilizing social media, addressing practical voting barriers, and forming strategic alliances—the Trump campaign can significantly enhance its voter turnout efforts, paving the way for a successful 2024 presidential run.

Engaging Trump's Base

Engaging Trump's base is a critical component of his strategy as he gears up for the 2024 presidential election. The foundation of this engagement lies in the deep-seated sentiments shared by his supporters, which are rooted in a desire for economic revitalization, robust national security, and a return to traditional values. To effectively mobilize this base, Trump must not only reaffirm his existing policies but also articulate a vision that resonates with the changing dynamics of the American electorate. This involves addressing the concerns of key demographics, including rural voters, working-class Americans, and those who feel left behind by globalization.

One of the pivotal aspects of Trump's approach is his economic policy, which emphasizes job creation, tax reforms, and trade agreements designed to benefit American workers. By promoting initiatives that prioritize domestic manufacturing and energy independence, Trump can appeal to voters disillusioned by previous administrations' policies that they perceive as favoring foreign interests over American jobs. Engaging his base means showcasing tangible results from his past policies while projecting a forward-looking agenda that promises to build on those successes. This economic narrative not only energizes his core supporters but also aims to attract undecided voters who prioritize economic stability.

Immigration reform remains another cornerstone of Trump's platform and an issue that galvanizes his base. His staunch advocacy for border security and a merit-based immigration system resonates with many Americans who associate immigration with job competition and cultural change. The 2024 campaign provides Trump with an opportunity to reiterate his commitment to these principles while addressing the evolving challenges at the border. By presenting clear, actionable proposals that promise to enhance national security and foster a legal immigration system, he can strengthen his appeal among constituents who view immigration as a critical issue.

The role of social media in Trump's engagement strategy cannot be overstated. His adept use of platforms like Twitter, Facebook, and Instagram allows him to communicate directly with his supporters, bypassing traditional media channels that often frame his message in a negative light. By crafting a narrative that emphasizes his accomplishments and critiques his opponents in real-time, Trump can maintain a strong connection with his base. This grassroots engagement, amplified through social media, not only fosters loyalty but also encourages his supporters to become active participants in the campaign, whether through sharing content, attending rallies, or volunteering.

In addition to social media, grassroots campaigning plays a crucial role in mobilizing Trump's base. The involvement of grassroots movements and local volunteer efforts can significantly enhance voter turnout, particularly in key swing states. By empowering his supporters to take ownership of the campaign through canvassing, phone banking, and organizing events, Trump cultivates a sense of community and shared purpose. Furthermore, strategic endorsements from influential figures and organizations can bolster his credibility and reach within specific voter segments. Ultimately, engaging Trump's base effectively requires a multifaceted approach that combines economic promises, immigration reform, social media outreach, and grassroots activism, all crucial to securing a successful 2024 presidential run.

The Use of Data Analytics in Mobilization

The integration of data analytics into political mobilization strategies represents a transformative shift in how campaigns are conducted, particularly in the context of Donald Trump's 2024 presidential run. This subchapter examines how data analytics not only enhances voter targeting but also optimizes resource allocation and campaign messaging. By leveraging vast amounts of voter data, campaigns can identify trends, preferences, and behaviors that inform strategic decisions, ultimately driving voter engagement and turnout. In an era where every vote counts, understanding the demographic nuances and political inclinations of specific voter groups becomes paramount.

Data analytics tools allow campaigns to segment the electorate with precision, identifying key demographics that align with Trump's policies and rhetoric. For instance, by analyzing previous voting patterns, socio-economic data, and even social media interactions, Trump's campaign can tailor its messaging to resonate with rural Americans, working-class voters, and those concerned about immigration and border security. This targeted approach not only speaks directly to the concerns of these groups but also fosters a sense of personal connection, which is crucial in mobilizing support. Additionally, data analytics enables the campaign to track the effectiveness of various outreach strategies, allowing for real-time adjustments that can maximize impact.

Moreover, the role of social media in conjunction with data analytics cannot be overstated. Trump's adept use of platforms like Twitter and Facebook exemplifies how data can inform content creation and dissemination. By analyzing engagement metrics and audience demographics, the campaign can craft messages that are more likely to go viral and engage supporters. This symbiotic relationship between data analytics and social media strategy not only amplifies Trump's message but also facilitates grassroots mobilization efforts, encouraging followers to take tangible actions such as attending rallies, volunteering, and spreading the campaign's narrative within their networks.

Grassroots movements, bolstered by data-driven insights, play a vital role in voter mobilization. The campaign can identify local influencers and community leaders who align with Trump's vision, empowering them to mobilize their networks effectively. By focusing on community-specific issues and leveraging data to inform these discussions, the campaign cultivates a grassroots momentum that is essential for energizing the base. This localized approach not only strengthens the campaign's presence on the ground but also reinforces the message that Trump is attuned to the needs and aspirations of everyday Americans.

In conclusion, the use of data analytics in mobilization strategies is a crucial component of Trump's 2024 campaign. It provides the tools necessary for understanding voter sentiment, optimizing outreach efforts, and engaging supporters through tailored messaging and grassroots initiatives. As the campaign progresses, the ability to harness data effectively will determine not only the success of mobilization efforts but also the broader narrative surrounding Trump's vision for America. The implications of these strategies extend beyond the campaign itself, shaping the future landscape of American politics and the expectations of how data can drive engagement in the electoral process.

Chapter 9: Opposition and Criticism

Responses from Political Opponents
Responses from political opponents to Donald Trump's immigration policies and the broader implications of his 2024 presidential run have been as varied as they are intense. In the wake of Trump's announcement to run for president again, critics from both the Democratic Party and some factions within the Republican Party have ramped up their critiques, framing his policies as divisive and detrimental to the fabric of American society. These opponents argue that Trump's hardline stance on immigration, characterized by increased border security and stringent enforcement measures, undermines the nation's foundational values of inclusivity and opportunity. They contend that such policies not only alienate immigrant communities but also fail to address the complexities of the modern immigration system.

Democratic leaders have made significant efforts to counter Trump's narrative by advocating for comprehensive immigration reform that emphasizes a pathway to citizenship for undocumented immigrants, protection for asylum seekers, and a humane approach to border security. They argue that Trump's focus on building walls and increasing deportations is a regressive strategy that overlooks the contributions of immigrants to the economy and society at large. This opposition has been amplified by various media outlets that have taken a critical stance on Trump's rhetoric and policies, often framing them as fear-mongering tactics designed to rally his base rather than implement effective solutions.

Within the Republican Party, some members have expressed concern over Trump's immigration agenda, fearing that it may alienate moderate voters and independents. These dissenting voices advocate for a more balanced approach that considers the economic contributions of immigrants while still addressing national security concerns. The internal conflict within the party has led to a reevaluation of strategies, as some Republicans attempt to carve out a platform that resonates with a broader electorate while still appealing to Trump's loyal supporters. This division underscores the complexities of navigating immigration issues in a politically charged environment.

Grassroots movements opposing Trump's policies have also gained momentum, mobilizing activists across the country to advocate for immigrant rights and challenge the narrative that equates immigration with crime and economic instability. These grassroots campaigns have utilized social media effectively to galvanize public support, increase awareness, and influence local and national discussions about immigration. The ability of these movements to organize rallies, fundraisers, and educational initiatives highlights the growing resistance to Trump's approach and the potential for a sustained counter-narrative to emerge in the upcoming election cycle.

As the 2024 campaign unfolds, the responses from political opponents will continue to play a critical role in shaping public perception and electoral outcomes. The juxtaposition of Trump's policies with alternative proposals from his opponents will not only influence voter sentiment but also inform the broader discourse on national identity, economic opportunity, and the role of immigration in American life. As both sides prepare for a contentious battle ahead, the implications of these responses will undoubtedly resonate throughout the campaign, impacting strategies, voter mobilization efforts, and ultimately, the future direction of American immigration policy.

Media Coverage and Public Perception

Media coverage plays a crucial role in shaping public perception, particularly in the context of political campaigns. As Donald Trump embarks on his 2024 presidential run, the narrative constructed by various media outlets will significantly influence how voters perceive his immigration policies and broader economic proposals. The media's framing of issues such as border security, job creation, and tax reforms can either bolster or undermine Trump's standing among key demographics. Understanding the interplay between media coverage and public sentiment is essential for grasping the dynamics of his campaign.

Throughout his political career, Trump has been adept at utilizing media, particularly social media, to engage his base and disseminate his message. His ability to bypass traditional media channels has allowed him to connect directly with supporters, shaping the narrative around his immigration policies in real-time. This direct engagement can create a sense of ownership among voters regarding his proposals, as they feel included in the conversation. However, it also invites scrutiny and criticism, as opponents leverage media platforms to challenge his assertions and mobilize dissent.

The portrayal of Trump's policies in the media often reflects broader societal attitudes toward immigration and economic reform. Positive coverage can reinforce perceptions of Trump as a decisive leader focused on national interests, resonating particularly with rural voters and those concerned about job security. Conversely, negative media portrayals can amplify fears and dissent, potentially alienating moderate voters. The duality of media narratives highlights the importance of strategic communication in shaping public perception and galvanizing support for Trump's campaign.

In addition to traditional and social media, the role of endorsements and grassroots campaigning cannot be overlooked. Influential figures and organizations lend credibility to Trump's policies, helping to shape media narratives that align with his vision. Grassroots movements, fueled by volunteer efforts, further enhance the reach of his message, creating a powerful synergy between media coverage and public mobilization. As voters become more engaged through these channels, their perceptions of Trump's immigration stance and economic proposals may solidify, influencing turnout at the polls.

Ultimately, the media's portrayal of Trump's campaign will be a pivotal factor in the 2024 election. As narratives evolve in response to his policies and public statements, the influence of media coverage on voter perception will become increasingly pronounced. For Republicans and policymakers alike, understanding the contours of this media landscape will be essential not only for crafting effective campaign strategies but also for anticipating the challenges they may face in translating public sentiment into electoral success.

Countering Criticism: Strategies and Tactics

Countering criticism is an essential aspect of political strategy, particularly for a figure as polarizing as Donald Trump. His 2024 presidential campaign faces scrutiny from various quarters, prompting the need for robust strategies and tactics to combat opposing narratives. Understanding how to effectively counter criticism can bolster support among constituents and maintain momentum in a competitive electoral landscape. This subchapter delves into the methods employed by Trump's campaign to address dissent and reinforce his message, thereby ensuring that his vision for America resonates with the electorate.

One of the primary tactics in countering criticism is the strategic use of social media. Trump's adeptness at leveraging platforms like Twitter and Facebook has allowed him to bypass traditional media narratives that often skew negative. By directly communicating with voters, he can frame issues on his terms and respond in real-time to critiques. This grassroots approach not only mobilizes his base but also cultivates a sense of loyalty and engagement among followers. Crafting messages that resonate emotionally and emphasize the perceived successes of his policies can effectively mitigate dissent and enhance voter enthusiasm.

In addition to social media engagement, establishing strong alliances and garnering endorsements plays a pivotal role in countering criticism. By aligning with influential figures and organizations, Trump's campaign can project an image of broad support and legitimacy. These endorsements serve to validate his policies and diminish the impact of dissenting voices. Highlighting endorsements from prominent Republican leaders, veterans, and grassroots organizations can reinforce his standing among key voter demographics, showcasing that his vision for America is not only popular but also widely accepted within the party.

Moreover, addressing opposition through targeted messaging is crucial. Trump's campaign can employ a dual strategy: directly challenging critics while simultaneously shifting the narrative to focus on policy achievements. By emphasizing economic growth, job creation, and tax reforms that benefit middle-class Americans, the campaign can redirect discussions away from negative portrayals. Incorporating success stories and testimonials from constituents who have benefited from his policies can humanize the campaign and strengthen its appeal. This approach not only counters criticism but also fosters a positive narrative that highlights the administration's accomplishments.

Finally, effective voter mobilization techniques are integral to countering criticism and ensuring electoral success. Engaging volunteers in grassroots efforts creates a formidable network that can disseminate favorable messages while counteracting dissent. The campaign can organize rallies, town halls, and community events that encourage interaction and foster a sense of community among supporters. These initiatives not only amplify Trump's message but also serve as a counter-narrative to media criticisms, showcasing the enthusiasm and dedication of his base. As a result, the campaign can cultivate a resilient voter bloc that feels empowered to advocate for Trump's vision and challenge opposing viewpoints.

In summary, countering criticism requires a multifaceted approach that combines social media strategy, strategic alliances, targeted messaging, and grassroots mobilization. By employing these tactics, Trump's 2024 campaign can navigate the complexities of opposition while reinforcing a cohesive and compelling narrative. As the electoral landscape continues to evolve, understanding and implementing these strategies will be crucial for maintaining support and driving voter engagement in the lead-up to the election.

Chapter 10: Historical Comparisons

Comparing Trump's 2024 Campaign to Previous Runs
Trump's 2024 campaign marks a significant evolution of his political strategy, building upon the foundation laid during his previous runs in 2016 and 2020. This campaign is characterized by a more refined focus on key issues that resonate with his base, particularly on economic policies, immigration reform, and voter mobilization techniques. While his core messaging remains anchored in the "Make America Great Again" mantra, the nuances of his approach reflect a response to the changing political landscape and the lessons learned from past electoral battles. A comparative analysis of these campaigns reveals both continuity and adaptation in strategy, particularly in how Trump seeks to engage voters and navigate the complexities of modern political discourse.

One of the most striking aspects of Trump's 2024 campaign is its emphasis on economic proposals. Drawing from his previous tenure, he revisits themes of job creation, tax reforms, and trade agreements, aiming to capitalize on the economic anxieties that have intensified in recent years. Unlike his earlier campaigns, where broad strokes defined his economic narrative, this time he presents detailed plans intended to address specific concerns such as inflation and supply chain disruptions. This shift not only aims to reassure voters of his competency in economic management but also seeks to differentiate his administration's achievements from the current administration's challenges, thereby reinforcing his appeal as a solution-oriented leader.

Immigration reform remains a cornerstone of Trump's campaign, reflecting his longstanding commitment to border security and stringent immigration policies. However, in 2024, there is a renewed focus on the implications of these policies for various voter demographics, particularly rural Americans who have felt the impacts of immigration firsthand. By framing his immigration stance as a means of protecting American jobs and enhancing community safety, Trump seeks to rally support from constituents who prioritize these issues. This strategy also responds to criticisms from opponents, positioning his policies not merely as enforcement measures but as essential for national stability and economic prosperity.

In the realm of digital engagement, Trump's use of social media has evolved into a sophisticated tool for voter mobilization. While his earlier campaigns relied on direct, often incendiary messaging to galvanize support, the 2024 campaign appears to adopt a more strategic approach to content dissemination. Trump's team utilizes targeted advertisements, influencer partnerships, and grassroots digital campaigns to reach specific voter segments, thereby enhancing engagement among younger voters and those disenchanted with traditional media. This adaptation reflects an understanding of the changing media landscape, where a nuanced social media strategy can significantly amplify voter outreach and mobilization efforts.

Endorsements and alliances have played a crucial role in shaping Trump's 2024 campaign narrative. By aligning with influential figures and organizations within the Republican Party, Trump not only consolidates his base but also reinforces his legitimacy as a frontrunner. The impact of these endorsements extends beyond mere political capital; they serve as a litmus test for party unity and loyalty among Republican voters. As Trump navigates opposition from both established politicians and media outlets, the strength of these alliances becomes increasingly vital in framing his campaign as a formidable force against perceived threats from the Democratic establishment. Together, these elements create a complex tapestry of strategies that distinguish Trump's 2024 campaign from his previous runs, while also reflecting broader trends in American political dynamics.

Lessons from Other Presidential Candidates

The history of presidential campaigns is replete with valuable lessons that can inform contemporary political strategies, particularly for candidates like Donald Trump in his 2024 run. By examining the successes and failures of past candidates, we can extract insights into effective messaging, voter engagement, and policy advocacy. From Richard Nixon's adept use of television to Barack Obama's groundbreaking social media strategy, the evolution of campaign dynamics offers a roadmap for navigating modern electoral challenges. Understanding these historical precedents is crucial for Trump's campaign, as it seeks to rally support and overcome the increasing complexities of contemporary voter demographics.

One significant lesson from past candidates is the power of a unifying message. For instance, Ronald Reagan's "Morning in America" campaign encapsulated a sense of optimism and hope that resonated deeply with voters during a time of economic struggle. Trump's 2024 campaign mirrors this approach with its emphasis on "Making America Great Again." However, it is essential for Trump to ensure that this message is not just a slogan but a comprehensive narrative that addresses the diverse concerns of the electorate. By focusing on job creation, tax reforms, and trade agreements, Trump can forge a connection with voters who feel economically marginalized, thereby expanding his base and enhancing his appeal.

Additionally, successful candidates have often maximized their grassroots campaigning efforts to mobilize support. For example, Bernie Sanders' campaigns highlighted the effectiveness of grassroots fundraising and volunteer mobilization in connecting with voters on a personal level. Trump's ability to harness grassroots movements could significantly impact his 2024 run, particularly in areas where traditional Republican support is waning. Engaging volunteers and fostering local initiatives can create a sense of ownership among constituents, thereby translating into higher voter turnout and loyalty at the polls.

Media strategy is another critical area where lessons from past candidates can be applied. The way candidates have navigated media landscapes has evolved dramatically, with social media now playing a central role in shaping public perception. Trump's previous campaign demonstrated the effectiveness of direct engagement with voters through platforms like Twitter and Facebook. However, as the media landscape becomes increasingly fragmented and polarized, it is paramount for Trump to refine his approach to ensure his messages are not only heard but also resonate positively with a broad audience. By strategically leveraging social media, Trump can counteract negative narratives while reinforcing his policy positions and campaign promises.

Finally, understanding the implications of endorsements and alliances can shape a candidate's trajectory. Historical campaigns have shown that key endorsements from influential figures can lend credibility and sway undecided voters. Trump's ability to secure endorsements from respected individuals and organizations within the Republican Party can bolster his campaign and encourage voter mobilization. It is essential for Trump to cultivate these relationships while also addressing opposition and criticism from political adversaries and media outlets. By learning from the past, Trump can better navigate the complex landscape of the 2024 election, ultimately enhancing his chances for success.

Historical Context of Immigration Policies

The historical context of immigration policies in the United States has evolved significantly over the decades, shaped by various political, social, and economic factors. Understanding this evolution is crucial for analyzing the current immigration landscape and how it influences contemporary political agendas, particularly those of the Republican Party. From the early restrictive measures of the Immigration Act of 1924 to the more lenient policies of the mid-20th century, each period reflects the prevailing attitudes towards immigration and the perceived impact on American society. This backdrop sets the stage for evaluating Trump's immigration policies and their implications for the 2024 presidential campaign.

In the latter half of the 20th century, immigration policy underwent significant transformations, particularly with the Immigration and Nationality Act of 1965, which eliminated national origin quotas and opened the door to a more diverse influx of immigrants. This change was largely influenced by civil rights movements advocating for equality and justice, signaling a shift in American values. However, as the demographics of the immigrant population changed, so too did the concerns among certain segments of the American populace, leading to a resurgence of nativist sentiments. These sentiments have often been leveraged by political figures, and Trump's 2016 campaign marked a notable resurgence in the focus on border security and immigration enforcement.

Trump's immigration policies, characterized by a hardline approach, can be viewed as a response to the perceived challenges posed by immigration, including economic competition and national security concerns. His administration implemented measures such as the travel ban targeting predominantly Muslim countries and the construction of a border wall, which became emblematic of his campaign. These policies were not merely reactive but part of a broader narrative that appealed to a base concerned about the impact of immigration on American jobs and culture. By framing immigration as a central issue, Trump has been able to galvanize support among voters who feel disenfranchised by the changes in immigration policy over the decades.

The implications of Trump's immigration stance extend beyond immediate policy outcomes; they have reshaped the Republican Party's platform and voter mobilization strategies. By emphasizing border security and stringent immigration controls, Trump has redefined what it means to be a Republican voter. This has fostered a grassroots movement that actively engages in volunteer efforts to promote his agenda and encourage voter turnout. The interplay between social media strategies and grassroots campaigning has become a critical component of how Trump communicates his message and connects with supporters, particularly younger voters who are increasingly influential in American politics.

As the 2024 campaign approaches, the historical context of immigration policies will continue to play a pivotal role in shaping electoral dynamics. Understanding the continuity and change in these policies helps elucidate the motivations behind Trump's current proposals and rhetoric. Furthermore, analyzing the responses from political opponents and media outlets reveals the contentious nature of immigration discourse in America. The interplay between historical precedents and current strategies will be essential in assessing how Trump navigates the complex landscape of immigration reform, voter mobilization, and public perception as he seeks to make America great again.

Chapter 11: Policy Impact on Key Demographics

Resonance with Rural Americans

Resonance with rural Americans is a pivotal theme in understanding the dynamics of Trump's immigration policies and broader campaign strategies. As the 2024 presidential election approaches, rural voters represent a significant demographic that has historically aligned itself with Trump's vision of America. This connection is rooted in a shared sense of identity, economic aspirations, and cultural values, which have become increasingly pronounced in the context of national debates on immigration and economic policy. For many rural Americans, Trump's advocacy for stronger border security and immigration reform aligns with their concerns about job security, wage stagnation, and the perceived erosion of community standards.

Trump's economic policies resonate deeply with rural constituencies, particularly his focus on job creation and tax reforms. Many rural areas have faced economic decline, exacerbated by global trade agreements that have not favored local industries. Trump's commitment to revitalizing manufacturing and agriculture, through targeted tax incentives and trade negotiations, speaks directly to the livelihoods of rural Americans. His administration's efforts to renegotiate trade deals, such as the USMCA, aimed to protect the agricultural sector from unfair competition, thereby reinforcing his appeal among voters who feel left behind by previous administrations.

Immigration reform remains a cornerstone of Trump's campaign, particularly in its implications for rural America. Many rural communities have experienced demographic shifts due to migration patterns, leading to both opportunities and challenges. Trump's hardline stance on immigration and border security resonates with voters who believe that unchecked immigration undermines local job markets and strains public resources. This perspective is often amplified by local narratives that emphasize the need for policies that prioritize American workers, thereby creating a sense of urgency and solidarity among rural voters who support stricter immigration controls.

The grassroots nature of Trump's campaigning strategies plays a critical role in mobilizing rural voters. His ability to harness the power of social media allows him to communicate directly with constituents, bypassing traditional media narratives that may not accurately represent their concerns. By engaging with rural communities through targeted messaging that reflects their values and experiences, Trump fosters a sense of belonging and empowerment. This grassroots approach not only amplifies his message but also encourages local volunteer efforts, creating a robust network of support that is vital for electoral success.

In evaluating the impact of endorsements and alliances on Trump's campaign, it is essential to consider how these factors resonate with rural Americans. Key endorsements from influential figures within agriculture, business, and local politics enhance Trump's credibility and reinforce his position as a champion of rural interests. As rural Americans assess the implications of their vote, they are often influenced by the endorsements that align with their values and priorities, solidifying their commitment to Trump's vision for America. As the 2024 election nears, understanding the intricate connections between Trump's policies and the sentiments of rural Americans will be crucial for both his campaign and the broader national discourse on immigration and economic reform.

Engaging Minority Voter Groups

Engaging minority voter groups presents a critical opportunity for the Republican Party as it seeks to broaden its appeal in the context of Trump's 2024 presidential campaign. Historically, minority communities have often leaned toward the Democratic Party, influenced by longstanding socio-economic issues and perceptions of inclusivity. However, as the political landscape evolves, there are substantial opportunities for Republicans to connect with these groups. By focusing on economic empowerment, addressing immigration concerns, and creating tailored outreach strategies, the GOP can foster a more inclusive narrative and ultimately enhance voter mobilization efforts among minorities.

The foundation of engaging minority voter groups lies in the effective communication of economic policies that resonate with their interests and needs. Trump's proposals for job creation, tax reforms, and trade agreements can be articulated in a manner that highlights their potential benefits for minority communities. For instance, initiatives aimed at promoting entrepreneurship and small business development can be particularly appealing, as they address issues of economic disparity and unemployment that disproportionately affect these populations. By showcasing success stories and emphasizing tangible outcomes from these policies, the Republican Party can begin to reshape its image and foster trust within minority communities.

Immigration reform is another pivotal area where Republicans can engage minority voters. Many minority groups have diverse perspectives on immigration policies, often shaped by their own experiences and backgrounds. A nuanced approach that acknowledges the importance of border security while also addressing the realities faced by immigrant communities can serve to bridge divides. By advocating for comprehensive reforms that prioritize legal immigration processes and workforce needs, the GOP can position itself as a party that values both security and compassion, thus appealing to a broader audience.

Grassroots campaigning will play a significant role in effectively engaging minority voters. Mobilizing local leaders and organizations within these communities can facilitate authentic conversations around the issues that matter most to them. Volunteer efforts that focus on building relationships rather than merely delivering campaign messages can create a sense of belonging and ownership among minority voters. This grassroots approach not only enhances voter turnout but also fosters a deeper understanding of the unique challenges faced by these groups, allowing the Republican Party to tailor its message accordingly.

Lastly, the importance of key endorsements and alliances cannot be overstated in the effort to engage minority voters. Support from influential figures within minority communities can lend credibility to the Republican message and help dispel misconceptions about the party. These endorsements should reflect a genuine commitment to addressing the concerns of minority voters, moving beyond token gestures to include meaningful policy discussions and community engagement. By strategically aligning with respected voices, the GOP can cultivate a narrative of inclusivity and shared purpose, ultimately strengthening its electoral prospects in the diverse electorate of 2024.

Analyzing the Impact of Policies on Specific Demographics

Analyzing the impact of Donald Trump's immigration policies on specific demographics reveals a complex interplay of economic, social, and political factors that shape voter sentiments. As the 2024 presidential campaign approaches, understanding how these policies resonate with various voter groups becomes crucial for both supporters and opponents. This analysis focuses on rural Americans, minorities, and suburban voters, each of whom has unique concerns and priorities that inform their perspectives on immigration and broader policy implications.

Rural Americans have historically been a significant demographic within the Republican base, and Trump's immigration policies have garnered mixed responses in these communities. Many rural voters express concerns about labor shortages in agriculture and other industries reliant on immigrant labor. Conversely, Trump's strong stance on border security appeals to those who prioritize national sovereignty and job protection. This dichotomy presents a challenge for the Trump campaign as it navigates the need to maintain support from rural constituents while addressing their economic anxieties regarding immigration. The effectiveness of Trump's messaging on job creation and border security will be critical in galvanizing this demographic.

Minorities, particularly Hispanic and Black voters, represent a vital sector in the electoral landscape. Trump's approach to immigration, characterized by its emphasis on enforcement and restriction, has often been critiqued for fostering division and fear among these groups. However, there is evidence that some segments of minority voters are receptive to Trump's economic policies, particularly those aimed at job creation and entrepreneurship. The challenge lies in balancing the perception of his immigration policies with the economic benefits he aims to deliver. Engaging with minority communities through targeted outreach and addressing their specific concerns regarding immigration could potentially shift perceptions and influence voter turnout.

Suburban voters present another critical demographic that the Trump campaign must consider. Historically, suburban areas have shown varying support for Republican candidates, often influenced by social issues, economic conditions, and local demographics. Trump's immigration policies, particularly those perceived as harsh, may alienate moderate suburban voters who prioritize inclusivity and community cohesion.

However, if the campaign can effectively communicate the economic advantages of immigration reform and border security, it may resonate with suburban residents concerned about safety and economic stability. Tailoring messages to highlight the positive impact of these policies on local economies could serve as a compelling strategy to win over this group.

In summary, analyzing the impact of Trump's immigration policies on specific demographics reveals both opportunities and challenges for his 2024 presidential campaign. By understanding the nuanced perspectives of rural Americans, minorities, and suburban voters, the campaign can craft targeted messages that resonate with these groups. As the political landscape evolves, the ability to effectively address the concerns and priorities of these demographics will play a crucial role in shaping the electoral outcome. Engaging in meaningful dialogue and demonstrating a commitment to policies that align with their interests could ultimately enhance voter mobilization and support for Trump's candidacy.

Chapter 12: Media Coverage and Narrative

The Media's Role in Shaping Public Perception

The media plays a pivotal role in shaping public perception, particularly in the context of political campaigns. As we approach the 2024 presidential election, Donald Trump's immigration policies and broader agenda are intricately woven into the narrative constructed by various media outlets. This subchapter examines the mechanisms through which the media influences public opinion, highlights the dichotomy between partisan coverage, and explores the implications of this dynamic on Trump's campaign strategies. Understanding this relationship is essential for grasping how perceptions are formed and shifted in the current political landscape, particularly among Republican voters and undecided constituents.

One of the most significant ways the media shapes public perception is through framing. The language and context used by journalists can influence how political issues, such as immigration and economic policies, are interpreted by the public. For instance, media outlets that focus on the humanitarian aspects of immigration may present Trump's policies as overly harsh, while those emphasizing border security might depict them as essential for national safety. This framing can significantly affect voter sentiment, making it crucial for Trump's campaign to actively engage with the narrative and counter opposing viewpoints. The strategic use of messaging in response to media coverage can thus serve as a powerful tool in swaying public opinion and galvanizing support.

Social media has emerged as a key battleground for shaping public perception, particularly for political figures like Trump. His adept use of platforms such as Twitter and Facebook allows him to bypass traditional media channels, directly communicating with supporters and disseminating his policies. This grassroots engagement is particularly relevant in a landscape where conventional media narratives may not align with his message. By creating a personal and direct line of communication, Trump can cultivate a loyal base of supporters who feel connected to his campaign. This approach not only reinforces his core message but also enables him to address and counteract negative portrayals propagated by mainstream media.

Moreover, media coverage influences voter mobilization efforts, particularly among Trump's base. As the narrative surrounding his campaign evolves, so too does the enthusiasm of his supporters. Positive media coverage can energize grassroots movements and volunteer efforts, whereas negative coverage may dampen turnout. Understanding this interplay is vital for strategizing voter mobilization techniques. Campaigns must not only focus on policy proposals but also on managing public perception through media engagement, ensuring that their messaging resonates with key demographics, including rural Americans and working-class voters who are crucial to Trump's electoral success.

Finally, the impact of key endorsements and alliances cannot be overlooked in the context of media narratives. Endorsements from influential figures can lend credibility to Trump's campaign and amplify positive coverage, while alliances with grassroots organizations can enhance voter outreach efforts. In a media landscape that often scrutinizes political maneuvers, the narrative surrounding these endorsements can significantly shape public perception. By strategically aligning with prominent voices and organizations, Trump's campaign can bolster its image and reinforce its messaging, ultimately influencing voter behavior as the election approaches. Understanding these dynamics is essential for comprehensively analyzing the role of media in shaping the public's perception of Trump's immigration policies and his broader vision for America.

Investigating Bias and Objectivity

Investigating bias and objectivity is crucial when analyzing the intricacies of Trump's immigration policies and their implications for the future of America. In an era characterized by polarized political discourse, understanding how various biases shape public perceptions and media narratives is essential for informed engagement among Republicans, government officials, students, and the general populace. This subchapter delves into the complexities of bias in reporting and commentary, particularly concerning immigration reform and Trump's broader political strategies, while emphasizing the importance of an objective lens in evaluating these developments.

The media landscape plays a significant role in shaping public opinion, and it often reflects inherent biases that can skew the perception of policies and political figures. For supporters of Trump's candidacy, the narrative frequently emphasizes his stance on border security and immigration reform as a means of protecting American jobs and maintaining national sovereignty. Conversely, critics often portray these policies as exclusionary and detrimental to America's multicultural identity. This dichotomy illustrates the necessity of scrutinizing the sources of information consumed by voters, as media outlets may prioritize sensationalism over balanced reporting. A critical examination of these narratives can enhance understanding of how they influence perceptions of Trump's immigration policies and their broader implications for his 2024 campaign.

In addition to media narratives, the role of social media in disseminating information and shaping public opinion cannot be overlooked. Trump's adept use of platforms like Twitter and Facebook allows him to communicate directly with his base, bypassing traditional media filters that may amplify bias. This direct line of communication fosters a sense of connection and loyalty among supporters but also raises questions about the veracity of the information shared. Investigating the effectiveness of Trump's social media strategy reveals how it serves not only as a tool for voter engagement but also as a vehicle for shaping narratives around immigration and economic policies. The need for critical assessment of content circulated on these platforms is paramount, as misinformation can distort public understanding of key issues.

Moreover, the investigation of bias extends to the grassroots movements supporting Trump's candidacy. These organizations often mobilize volunteers and resources to promote his policies, particularly in areas heavily impacted by immigration. However, the narratives crafted by these grassroots efforts can sometimes overlook counterpoints or alternative perspectives. By analyzing the motivations and messaging behind grassroots campaigns, we can gain insight into the ways in which bias manifests in local and national efforts to rally support for Trump. This understanding is crucial for evaluating how these movements affect voter mobilization and the overall electoral landscape.

Finally, the exploration of key endorsements and alliances further illustrates the intricacies of bias and objectivity in the context of Trump's 2024 campaign. Endorsements from influential figures can lend credibility to Trump's policies and bolster his appeal among certain voter demographics. However, the motivations behind these endorsements and the potential biases of the endorsers must be scrutinized to fully appreciate their impact on the campaign. By fostering an environment where critical thinking prevails over blind allegiance, we can better navigate the complex interplay of bias, objectivity, and political strategy, ultimately contributing to a more informed electorate prepared to engage with the pressing issues of our time.

The Influence of Media on Trump's Electoral Success

The 2016 presidential election marked a significant turning point in the relationship between media and political campaigns, particularly for Donald Trump. His adept use of various media channels, especially social media, not only shaped his public persona but also played a crucial role in mobilizing his base. Trump's ability to communicate directly with voters through platforms like Twitter allowed him to bypass traditional media filters, fostering a sense of authenticity and immediacy that resonated with many Americans disillusioned by conventional political discourse. This direct engagement enabled him to frame the narrative surrounding his candidacy and policies, particularly concerning immigration, which became a cornerstone of his campaign.

As Trump embarks on his 2024 presidential run, examining the media's role in his electoral success reveals a complex interplay between message control and public perception. The narrative crafted by both Trump and the media has significant implications for his immigration policies, which continue to be a focal point of his campaign. His administration's hardline stance on border security and immigration reform was often amplified by media coverage, which both criticized and supported various aspects of his policies. This duality in representation has shaped the perceptions of voters, particularly among those who prioritize immigration issues, illustrating how media narratives can sway public opinion and electoral outcomes.

In addition to traditional news outlets, Trump's strategic use of social media has fundamentally altered voter engagement techniques. By leveraging platforms to disseminate his message, he has effectively engaged younger voters and those who may feel alienated by conventional political platforms. Trump's tweets and online posts often prioritize immediacy and emotional resonance over nuanced policy discussions, appealing to a demographic that values authenticity and direct communication. This strategy has proven effective in mobilizing his base, ensuring that his supporters remain engaged and energized as he approaches the 2024 election.

Moreover, media coverage of Trump's endorsements and alliances has also influenced his electoral success. High-profile endorsements from influential figures and organizations not only lend credibility to his campaign but also attract media attention, further amplifying his message. The media's focus on these endorsements can create an impression of momentum and legitimacy, which is critical in shaping voter perceptions. In a political landscape where image plays a vital role, the ability to garner support from respected entities can significantly bolster a candidate's standing in the eyes of potential voters.

Lastly, the ongoing criticism and opposition from various media outlets serve to reinforce Trump's narrative of being an outsider fighting against a biased system. This portrayal resonates deeply with many voters who feel marginalized by traditional political structures. The media's coverage of Trump's 2024 campaign, whether critical or supportive, ultimately shapes the electoral landscape, influencing voter mobilization efforts and engagement strategies. As Trump continues to navigate this complex media environment, understanding the influence of media on his electoral success will be essential for both his campaign and the broader implications for American politics.

Chapter 13: Conclusion

Summary of Key Findings

The subchapter "Summary of Key Findings" encapsulates the pivotal discoveries regarding Donald Trump's immigration policies and their broader implications for the future of America, particularly in the context of his 2024 presidential campaign. The analysis reveals a multifaceted approach to immigration that intertwines with broader economic strategies, social media engagement, grassroots mobilization, and the dynamics of voter sentiment. Understanding these elements is crucial for Republicans, government officials, and students of political science as they navigate the complexities of contemporary American political discourse.

One of the key findings highlights Trump's unwavering emphasis on border security as a cornerstone of his immigration policy. This focus has not only resonated with his base but has also been instrumental in shaping public opinion on immigration issues. The correlation between enhanced border security measures and perceptions of national safety has become a rallying point for many voters. As Trump prepares for the 2024 campaign, his stance on immigration continues to signify a commitment to prioritizing American sovereignty and safety, which is expected to play a significant role in mobilizing support among conservative constituents.

Economic policies proposed by Trump are intrinsically linked to his immigration agenda. The analysis identifies a direct relationship between immigration reform and job creation strategies. By advocating for policies that favor skilled immigration and workforce alignment, Trump aims to bolster the economy while addressing labor shortages in critical sectors. This dual approach not only appeals to business interests but also serves as a mechanism for appealing to voters concerned about economic stability and job availability. The effectiveness of these proposals in driving voter turnout will be a crucial factor in the upcoming election.

Social media strategy emerges as another vital component of Trump's campaign framework. The findings illustrate how Trump leverages platforms like Twitter and Facebook to communicate directly with voters, circumventing traditional media filters. His ability to engage audiences, disseminate his policies, and respond to criticism in real time has transformed the landscape of modern campaigning. This strategy not only amplifies his message but also fosters a sense of community among supporters, which is essential for grassroots campaigning efforts that are integral to his electoral strategy.

Finally, the examination of endorsements and alliances reveals their significant impact on Trump's campaign. Key endorsements from influential figures and organizations lend credibility to his candidacy and amplify his messaging. The findings also suggest that these alliances can help mitigate opposition and criticism from political adversaries and the media. Understanding how these endorsements shape public perception and voter mobilization will be critical for strategists and supporters as they navigate the complexities of the 2024 electoral landscape. By synthesizing these key findings, stakeholders can better appreciate the intricate interplay of immigration policy, economic strategy, and voter engagement that defines Trump's approach as he seeks to make America great again.

The Future of Trump's Immigration Policies

The future of Trump's immigration policies is poised to be a defining aspect of his 2024 presidential campaign, reflecting a commitment to border security and a reassessment of immigration reform. As he seeks to galvanize his base and attract undecided voters, Trump is likely to continue emphasizing the importance of a robust immigration system that prioritizes American interests. This approach aligns with his previous policies, which were characterized by strict enforcement measures, including the construction of a border wall and the implementation of travel bans targeting specific countries. In this context, Trump's narrative will likely focus on national security, economic stability, and the preservation of American jobs as central themes.

In the realm of economic policies, Trump's immigration stance is intricately linked to his proposals for job creation and tax reforms. By advocating for stringent immigration controls, he positions himself as a defender of American workers, arguing that unchecked immigration can lead to job displacement and wage suppression. This rhetoric resonates particularly well with rural and working-class voters who feel economically marginalized. In shaping his message for the

2024 campaign, Trump may propose policies that not only bolster border security but also create pathways for legal immigration that align with labor market needs, thereby appealing to both sides of the immigration debate.

Social media strategy will play a crucial role in disseminating Trump's immigration message and engaging voters. His adept use of platforms like Twitter and Facebook allows him to communicate directly with his audience, bypassing traditional media filters. By leveraging social media, Trump can share success stories related to his immigration policies, highlight perceived failures of his opponents, and mobilize grassroots support. This direct engagement is essential for maintaining enthusiasm among his base, especially among younger voters who consume information predominantly through digital channels. The effectiveness of this strategy will be critical in shaping public perception and influencing voter turnout.

Grassroots campaigning will further amplify Trump's immigration agenda. By fostering a network of volunteers and local supporters, he can build a robust ground game that emphasizes community involvement and activism. These grassroots movements not only mobilize voters but also serve to reinforce Trump's narrative around immigration, creating a sense of urgency and shared purpose among supporters. The campaign's ability to harness this grassroots energy will be vital in counteracting opposition and criticism from political adversaries and mainstream media, which often portray his immigration policies in a negative light.

Ultimately, the implications of Trump's immigration policies will extend beyond the 2024 campaign, shaping the future landscape of American immigration. As he navigates the complexities of voter demographics and public sentiment, Trump's policies will have to balance the demands for security with the realities of a globalized economy. The effectiveness of his immigration strategy will be measured not just in electoral success, but also in its impact on key demographics, including minorities and urban voters. By addressing these challenges head-on, Trump can solidify his position as a leading voice on immigration, setting the stage for a transformative approach that could redefine America's relationship with immigration in the years to come.

Implications for America's Political Landscape

The implications of Trump's immigration policies on America's political landscape are profound and multifaceted, significantly shaping the discourse leading into the 2024 presidential election. As discussions about border security, legal immigration pathways, and enforcement intensify, they have become pivotal issues that resonate across various voter demographics. For Republicans, these policies are not just about immigration; they encapsulate broader themes of national identity, economic stability, and security. The framing of immigration in the context of "Making America Great Again" serves to reinforce a narrative that appeals to a significant portion of the electorate, underscoring the importance of these policies in the upcoming campaign.

Trump's approach to immigration reform has also sparked a vigorous debate regarding the economic implications of his proposals. Advocating for stricter border controls and adjustments to legal immigration channels, Trump positions these policies as essential for job creation and preserving

American wages. This stance resonates particularly with blue-collar workers and rural voters who perceive immigration as a threat to their economic security. As Trump articulates plans for tax reforms and trade agreements, his immigration policies are intertwined with a broader economic strategy aimed at galvanizing support among those who feel left behind in the current economic landscape. Consequently, immigration becomes a lens through which voters evaluate the effectiveness of Republican economic policies.

Social media has emerged as a critical tool in Trump's campaign strategy, allowing him to engage directly with voters and shape public discourse around immigration. By leveraging platforms such as Twitter and Facebook, Trump disseminates his message and counteracts criticisms in real-time, effectively mobilizing his base. This grassroots approach is particularly relevant as it fosters a sense of community among supporters who are passionate about immigration issues. The ability to rally voters through targeted messaging and personal anecdotes about immigration reinforces the emotional underpinnings of his campaign, making it a potent element of his political strategy as he seeks to maintain enthusiasm among his supporters.

Endorsements and alliances play a significant role in amplifying Trump's messaging on immigration. Influential figures and organizations that align with his views on border security lend credibility and visibility to his campaign, impacting voter perceptions and mobilization efforts. These endorsements bolster the narrative that Trump's immigration policies have widespread support within the Republican Party, creating a unified front that can sway undecided voters. As

Trump navigates the complexities of coalition-building, the implications of these relationships extend beyond the election, potentially shaping the future direction of Republican policies on immigration.

The media's portrayal of Trump's immigration policies and broader campaign strategy also influences public perception and voter behavior. Coverage of his policies can either reinforce or challenge the narratives he seeks to promote, affecting how different demographics engage with his message. By examining historical comparisons to previous presidential campaigns, it becomes evident that media coverage plays a critical role in framing the issues at stake, from immigration to economic policy. As Trump continues to cultivate his brand and message in the lead-up to the 2024 election, understanding these dynamics will be essential for both his supporters and opponents as they navigate the evolving political landscape.

Chapter 14: Judicial Appointments and Legal Influence

The judicial appointments made during Trump's administration represent a profound and lasting impact on the American legal system. His strategic focus on appointing conservative judges reshaped the judiciary, ensuring that conservative principles would influence U.S. law for generations to come. Trump's appointment of over 230 federal judges, including three Supreme Court justices—Neil Gorsuch, Brett Kavanaugh, and Amy Coney Barrett—solidified a conservative majority on the Supreme Court. This shift is not merely a reflection of political strategy but a commitment to preserving constitutional integrity as understood by originalist and textualist philosophies.

The Significance of Supreme Court Appointments

The Supreme Court plays a crucial role in interpreting the Constitution and can significantly influence the direction of U.S. law. Trump's appointments to the Court have already begun to affect decisions on critical issues such as abortion, gun rights, religious freedom, and executive power. For instance, the overturning of *Roe v. Wade* by the Court in *Dobbs v. Jackson*

Women's Health Organization was a direct result of the conservative majority Trump helped establish. This decision returned the power to regulate abortion to the states, a move applauded by many conservatives as a victory for states' rights and the protection of unborn lives.

In contrast, Kamala Harris has consistently supported judicial appointments that reflect a more progressive agenda, advocating for judges who interpret the Constitution in a manner that evolves with contemporary social issues. Her stance is seen by many conservatives as a departure from the original intent of the Founders, risking the erosion of fundamental rights and principles.

Federal Appellate and District Courts

Beyond the Supreme Court, Trump's influence extended to the federal appellate courts, where he appointed 54 judges to lifetime positions. These courts often have the final say on many legal issues, as the Supreme Court hears only a small percentage of cases. The impact of these appointments is already being felt in decisions related to immigration, healthcare, and administrative law. For example, Trump-appointed judges have played key roles in upholding the administration's immigration policies and in striking down overreaching regulations imposed by federal agencies.

The Trump administration's judicial appointments were characterized by their emphasis on youth and ideological consistency. By appointing younger judges, Trump ensured that his judicial philosophy would persist for decades. Many of these judges were selected from lists prepared by the Federalist Society, a conservative legal organization dedicated to promoting a textualist and originalist interpretation of the Constitution.

Kamala Harris's Judicial Philosophy

In contrast, Kamala Harris's approach to judicial appointments would likely emphasize diversity and progressive interpretations of the law. Her judicial philosophy is rooted in the belief that the Constitution is a living document, one that should be interpreted in light of contemporary values and social justice concerns. This approach, while appealing to some, is viewed by many conservatives as a threat to the rule of law and the stability of legal precedents.

Harris has also been a vocal critic of Trump's judicial appointments, arguing that they are out of step with the needs of a modern, diverse society. She has advocated for the appointment of judges who would protect reproductive rights, LGBTQ+ rights, and environmental regulations. However, critics argue that her approach would lead to judicial activism, where judges impose their personal views rather than adhering to the law as written.

Global Implications of U.S. Judicial Philosophy

The U.S. legal system is often seen as a model for the world, and changes in the judiciary can have global repercussions. A judiciary that adheres to a strict interpretation of the Constitution provides predictability and stability, which are crucial for international business and diplomacy. Trump's judicial appointments have been praised for reinforcing the rule of law and for providing a counterbalance to what many see as the overreach of the administrative state.

Kamala Harris's judicial philosophy, on the other hand, could introduce uncertainty into the legal system. If judges are seen as making decisions based on evolving social norms rather than established legal principles, it could undermine confidence in the U.S. legal system. This uncertainty could have negative implications for global trade and investment, as businesses rely on a stable and predictable legal environment.

Conclusion: The Case for Trump's Judicial Appointments

In conclusion, Trump's judicial appointments represent a significant and lasting legacy that reinforces conservative values and the rule of law. These appointments are crucial not only for maintaining a balanced judiciary but also for ensuring that the U.S. legal system remains a model for the world. In contrast, Kamala Harris's approach to judicial appointments could lead to greater judicial activism and uncertainty, both domestically and globally. For those who value a judiciary that adheres to the Constitution and provides a stable legal environment, Trump's judicial legacy is a compelling reason to support his re-election in November 2024.

Chapter 15: Foreign Policy and International Relations

Donald Trump's foreign policy was characterized by a radical departure from the traditional diplomatic strategies of past administrations. His approach was defined by a strong emphasis on American sovereignty, economic nationalism, and a willingness to challenge the status quo in international relations. The "America First" doctrine that guided Trump's foreign policy was aimed at prioritizing U.S. interests in every international engagement, often at the expense of multilateral agreements and alliances.

Trade Policies and Economic Nationalism

One of the cornerstones of Trump's foreign policy was his approach to trade. Trump viewed existing trade agreements as detrimental to American workers and industries, believing that they allowed other countries to take advantage of the U.S. His administration renegotiated several key trade agreements, most notably replacing NAFTA with the United States-Mexico-Canada Agreement (USMCA). The USMCA was designed to provide better terms for American workers and to correct what Trump saw as the deficiencies of NAFTA, which he claimed had led to the loss of millions of American manufacturing jobs.

Trump also initiated a trade war with China, imposing tariffs on hundreds of billions of dollars' worth of Chinese goods. This move was intended to address the massive trade deficit between the U.S. and China and to push back against what Trump saw as China's unfair trade practices, including intellectual property theft and forced technology transfers. The tariffs were controversial, as they led to retaliatory tariffs from China and disrupted global supply chains. However, many of Trump's supporters argue that these actions were necessary to protect American industries and to stand up to China's growing economic influence.

Kamala Harris, in contrast, has criticized Trump's trade policies, arguing that they have hurt American consumers and farmers. She has advocated for a more cooperative approach to international trade, one that involves working with allies to address issues like intellectual property theft and climate change. However, critics of Harris's approach argue that it would result in the U.S. making concessions that would weaken its economic position and make it more dependent on international institutions that do not always have America's best interests at heart.

Diplomatic Relations and Global Leadership

Trump's foreign policy was also marked by a reevaluation of America's role in the world. He questioned the value of long-standing alliances and international organizations, arguing that they often benefited other countries at the expense of the U.S. For example, Trump was a vocal critic of NATO, insisting that member countries needed to pay their fair share for defense. This stance led to tensions within the alliance, with some leaders questioning America's commitment to NATO's collective defense principle.

However, Trump's willingness to challenge international norms also led to significant diplomatic breakthroughs. His administration brokered the Abraham Accords, which normalized relations between Israel and several Arab nations. This was a major achievement in Middle Eastern diplomacy and represented a significant shift in the region's political landscape. Trump's direct engagement with North Korea, while controversial, also represented a departure from the strategies of previous administrations and brought attention to the denuclearization of the Korean Peninsula.

Kamala Harris's approach to foreign policy is likely to be more in line with traditional U.S. diplomacy, emphasizing the importance of alliances and multilateral cooperation. Harris has indicated that she would rejoin the Iran nuclear deal and recommit the U.S. to the Paris Climate Agreement. However, critics argue that her approach could weaken America's negotiating position and result in the U.S. making concessions that could undermine its global leadership.

Global Impact of Foreign Policy Decisions

The foreign policy decisions made by the U.S. have far-reaching implications for the global economy and international relations. Trump's emphasis on economic nationalism and his willingness to challenge international norms have led to a reevaluation of global trade practices and alliances. His administration's hardline stance on China, in particular, has highlighted the growing competition between the two superpowers and has forced other countries to consider their own positions in this new global landscape.

Kamala Harris's foreign policy, in contrast, would likely involve a return to more traditional diplomacy, with an emphasis on rebuilding alliances and working within international institutions. While this approach might reduce tensions with allies, it could also result in a less assertive U.S. on the global stage, potentially allowing countries like China and Russia to expand their influence.

Conclusion: The Case for Trump's Foreign Policy

Trump's foreign policy represents a bold reassertion of American sovereignty and a willingness to challenge the global status quo. His actions on trade, diplomacy, and international relations were guided by a desire to put America's interests first, even when it meant challenging long-standing alliances and agreements. In contrast, Kamala Harris's approach to foreign policy would likely involve a return to the strategies of past administrations, with an emphasis on multilateralism and cooperation.

For those who believe that America must prioritize its own interests and take a more assertive role in the world, Trump's foreign policy is a compelling reason to support his re-election. The stakes in the 2024 election are high, not just for the U.S. but for the entire world, as the decisions made by the next administration will shape the global landscape for years to come.

Chapter 16: Economic Policies and Job Creation

Donald Trump's economic policies were centered around the belief that reducing government intervention and fostering a pro-business environment would lead to economic growth and job creation. His administration implemented significant tax cuts, deregulation, and trade policies designed to boost American industries and workers. The results, according to his supporters, were a booming economy and record-low unemployment rates before the COVID-19 pandemic disrupted global markets.

Tax Cuts and Jobs Act

One of the most significant achievements of the Trump administration was the passage of the Tax Cuts and Jobs Act (TCJA) in 2017. The TCJA lowered the corporate tax rate from 35% to 21%, making it one of the most competitive rates among developed nations. The act also provided tax cuts for individuals, doubled the standard deduction, and eliminated the individual mandate penalty from the Affordable Care Act.

Proponents of the TCJA argue that these tax cuts stimulated economic growth by encouraging businesses to invest in the U.S. economy. The reduction in the corporate tax rate, in particular, was seen as a major incentive for companies to bring jobs and capital back to the U.S. Supporters also point to the repatriation of overseas profits and the resulting increase in business investment as evidence that the tax cuts were effective in boosting the economy.

Kamala Harris, however, has been a vocal critic of the TCJA, arguing that it disproportionately benefited the wealthy and large corporations at the expense of middle- and lower-income Americans. She has advocated for rolling back the corporate tax cuts and increasing taxes on the wealthy to fund social programs and infrastructure projects. Critics of Harris's approach argue that raising taxes on businesses would stifle economic growth, lead to job losses, and make the U.S. less competitive globally.

Deregulation and Its Impact on the Economy

Another key aspect of Trump's economic policy was his focus on deregulation. The Trump administration rolled back numerous regulations across various sectors, including energy, finance, and environmental protection. The goal was to reduce the burden of government regulations on businesses, which Trump argued were stifling innovation and economic growth.

One of the most significant deregulation efforts was in the energy sector, where the Trump administration reversed many of the Obama-era regulations on fossil fuels. This included opening up federal lands for oil and gas drilling, rolling back restrictions on coal production, and withdrawing from the Paris Climate Agreement. These actions were intended to promote energy independence and create jobs in the energy sector.

Critics, including Kamala Harris, argue that Trump's deregulation efforts prioritized corporate profits over environmental protection and public health. Harris has been a strong advocate for reintroducing and strengthening environmental regulations, including rejoining the Paris Climate Agreement and transitioning the U.S. to a clean energy economy. However, opponents of Harris's approach argue that her environmental policies would lead to job losses in traditional energy sectors and increase energy costs for consumers.

Job Creation and the Pre-Pandemic Economy

Under Trump's administration, the U.S. economy experienced significant job growth, with unemployment rates reaching historic lows for all demographic groups, including African Americans, Hispanics, and women. The economic boom was attributed to the pro-business policies implemented by the administration, including tax cuts and deregulation.

The administration also focused on revitalizing American manufacturing, with Trump frequently highlighting the importance of bringing jobs back to the U.S. from overseas. The renegotiation of trade deals, such as the USMCA, was part of this effort to protect American workers and industries from unfair competition.

Kamala Harris has argued that while the pre-pandemic economy may have been strong, it was not inclusive, and many Americans were still struggling with income inequality, lack of access to healthcare, and job insecurity. She has proposed policies aimed at addressing these issues, including raising the minimum wage, expanding access to healthcare, and investing in education and job training programs.

However, critics of Harris's economic proposals argue that they would lead to increased government intervention in the economy, higher taxes, and more regulations, which could stifle economic growth and lead to job losses.

Global Implications of U.S. Economic Policies

The U.S. economy plays a central role in the global economy, and the policies implemented by the U.S. government have far-reaching implications for global markets. Trump's economic policies, particularly his trade policies, were designed to protect American industries from unfair competition and to reduce the U.S. trade deficit. His administration's tough stance on China, including the imposition of tariffs, was seen as a necessary step to address the growing economic and geopolitical threat posed by China.

Kamala Harris's economic policies, in contrast, are likely to involve greater cooperation with international institutions and a focus on addressing global challenges such as climate change and income inequality. However, critics argue that her approach could lead to increased reliance on global supply chains, which could make the U.S. more vulnerable to economic disruptions and reduce its ability to compete globally.

Conclusion: The Case for Trump's Economic Policies

In conclusion, Trump's economic policies were designed to prioritize American workers and industries, reduce government intervention in the economy, and promote economic growth. The results, according to his supporters, were a strong economy and record-low unemployment rates before the pandemic. In contrast, Kamala Harris's economic proposals are seen by critics as likely to lead to increased taxes, more regulations, and greater government intervention, which could stifle economic growth and lead to job losses.

For those who believe that a strong, pro-business environment is essential for economic growth and job creation, Trump's economic policies are a compelling reason to support his re-election. The stakes in the 2024 election are high, not just for the U.S. economy but for the global economy as well, as the policies implemented by the next administration will have far-reaching implications for global markets.

Chapter 17: Healthcare Policies and the Future of American Healthcare

Healthcare has been one of the most contentious issues in American politics, and the Trump administration's approach to healthcare was marked by efforts to repeal and replace the Affordable Care Act (ACA), also known as Obamacare. Trump's healthcare policies were aimed at reducing government intervention in the healthcare system, increasing competition, and providing more choices for consumers.

Efforts to Repeal and Replace the ACA

One of Trump's key campaign promises in 2016 was to repeal and replace the ACA, which he and many Republicans argued was a failed policy that led to rising healthcare costs and reduced choices for consumers. The administration made several attempts to repeal the ACA, but these efforts were ultimately unsuccessful in Congress.

Despite the failure to repeal the ACA, the Trump administration took several actions to weaken the law. This included eliminating the individual mandate penalty, which required individuals to purchase health insurance or face a tax penalty. The elimination of the individual mandate was seen by many as a significant blow to the ACA, as it reduced the incentive for healthy individuals to purchase insurance, leading to higher premiums for those who remained in the market.

Kamala Harris has been a strong supporter of the ACA and has advocated for expanding the law to provide healthcare coverage to more Americans. She has also supported proposals for a single-payer healthcare system, commonly referred to as "Medicare for All." Harris argues that healthcare is a fundamental right and that the government should play a larger role in ensuring that all Americans have access to affordable healthcare.

Critics of Harris's approach argue that a single-payer system would lead to increased government control over healthcare, reduce competition, and result in higher taxes to pay for the program. They also argue that it would lead to longer wait times for medical services and reduce the quality of care.

Deregulation and Healthcare Innovation

In addition to efforts to repeal the ACA, the Trump administration focused on deregulating the healthcare industry to promote innovation and reduce costs. This included initiatives to expand the availability of short-term health plans, which are less expensive but offer fewer benefits than ACA-compliant plans. The administration also promoted the use of health savings accounts (HSAs) and association health plans (AHPs), which allow small businesses to band together to purchase health insurance at lower rates.

Supporters of these policies argue that they provide consumers with more choices and allow individuals and businesses to find health plans that best meet their needs. They also argue that deregulation promotes competition in the healthcare market, which can lead to lower costs and increased innovation.

Kamala Harris has criticized these efforts, arguing that they undermine the protections provided by the ACA and leave consumers with substandard health coverage. She has advocated for stronger regulations to ensure that all Americans have access to comprehensive healthcare coverage.

Prescription Drug Prices and Healthcare Costs

Reducing the cost of prescription drugs was another priority for the Trump administration. Trump frequently criticized the pharmaceutical industry for high drug prices and took several actions to address the issue. This included allowing states to import prescription drugs from Canada, where prices are often lower, and implementing a "most favored nation" rule, which would tie the prices of certain drugs in the U.S. to the lower prices paid in other developed countries.

The administration also worked to increase transparency in healthcare pricing, requiring hospitals to disclose the prices they charge for various services. Supporters of these efforts argue that greater transparency and competition are essential for reducing healthcare costs and making healthcare more affordable for Americans.

Kamala Harris has also advocated for reducing prescription drug prices, but her approach involves more government intervention. She has supported allowing Medicare to negotiate drug prices directly with pharmaceutical companies and has proposed capping the price of prescription drugs. Harris argues that the government needs to take a more active role in regulating drug prices to protect consumers from price gouging.

Critics of Harris's approach argue that price controls could stifle innovation in the pharmaceutical industry and lead to reduced investment in research and development. They also argue that allowing the government to negotiate drug prices could lead to shortages and reduce access to life-saving medications.

The Future of American Healthcare

The future of American healthcare is a central issue in the 2024 election, with stark differences between the policies proposed by Trump and Harris. Trump's approach is based on reducing government intervention, promoting competition, and providing more choices for consumers. His supporters argue that these policies will lead to lower costs and increased innovation in the healthcare industry.

In contrast, Kamala Harris advocates for a more significant role for the government in healthcare, with a focus on expanding access to coverage and ensuring that all Americans have access to affordable healthcare. Her critics argue that her policies would lead to higher taxes, reduced competition, and lower quality of care.

Conclusion: The Case for Trump's Healthcare Policies

In conclusion, Trump's healthcare policies were designed to reduce government intervention in the healthcare system, increase competition, and provide more choices for consumers. His supporters argue that these policies are essential for reducing healthcare costs and promoting innovation in the healthcare industry. In contrast, Kamala Harris's healthcare proposals are seen by critics as likely to lead to increased government control, higher taxes, and reduced quality of care.

For those who believe that a free-market approach is essential for a sustainable and effective healthcare system, Trump's policies provide a compelling reason to support his re-election. The 2024 election will have significant implications for the future of American healthcare, and the policies implemented by the next administration will determine the direction of the healthcare system for years to come.

Chapter 18: Foreign Policy and National Security

Donald Trump's foreign policy was characterized by a focus on "America First," with an emphasis on protecting American interests, reducing the U.S. involvement in foreign conflicts, and renegotiating trade deals to benefit American workers. His administration took a tough stance on China, withdrew from several international agreements, and sought to bring American troops home from overseas conflicts.

The "America First" Doctrine

The "America First" doctrine was central to Trump's foreign policy, with a focus on protecting American interests and reducing the U.S. involvement in foreign conflicts. Trump argued that the U.S. had been taken advantage of by other countries for too long and that it was time to prioritize American workers and industries.

This approach was evident in Trump's decision to withdraw from the Trans-Pacific Partnership (TPP), renegotiate the North American Free Trade Agreement (NAFTA), and impose tariffs on Chinese goods. Supporters of these actions argue that they were necessary to protect

American jobs and industries from unfair competition and to reduce the U.S. trade deficit.

Kamala Harris, on the other hand, has criticized Trump's "America First" approach, arguing that it has alienated U.S. allies and weakened the country's leadership on the global stage. Harris has advocated for re-engaging with international institutions, rebuilding alliances, and addressing global challenges such as climate change and human rights.

Critics of Harris's approach argue that her focus on global cooperation could lead to the U.S. being taken advantage of by other countries and could reduce the country's ability to protect its own interests. They also argue that her emphasis on global challenges such as climate change could lead to policies that prioritize international concerns over American workers and industries.

China and the Trade War

One of the most significant aspects of Trump's foreign policy was his tough stance on China. The administration imposed tariffs on Chinese goods, accused China of unfair trade practices, and sought to reduce the U.S. trade deficit with China. Trump also took steps to address concerns about Chinese influence in the U.S., including banning Chinese technology companies such as Huawei from participating in the U.S. market.

Supporters of Trump's approach argue that China poses a significant economic and geopolitical threat to the U.S. and that tough measures are necessary to protect American interests. They also argue that the tariffs were effective in pressuring China to make concessions in trade negotiations and in reducing the U.S. trade deficit.

Kamala Harris has been critical of Trump's approach to China, arguing that the trade war has hurt American farmers and businesses and has not led to significant changes in China's behavior. Harris has advocated for a more cooperative approach to China, with a focus on addressing global challenges such as climate change and human rights.

Critics of Harris's approach argue that a more cooperative stance towards China could lead to the U.S. being taken advantage of and could reduce the country's ability to protect its own interests. They also argue that Harris's focus on global challenges could lead to policies that prioritize international concerns over American workers and industries.

Middle East Policy and the Abraham Accords

Trump's foreign policy in the Middle East was marked by the signing of the Abraham Accords, a series of agreements between Israel and several Arab countries to normalize relations. The accords were seen as a significant achievement in promoting peace and stability in the region and were widely praised by Trump's supporters.

The administration also took a tough stance on Iran, withdrawing from the Iran nuclear deal and imposing sanctions on the country. Trump argued that the deal was flawed and that Iran was not living up to its commitments. The administration's goal was to pressure Iran into renegotiating the deal and to reduce its influence in the region.

Kamala Harris has been critical of Trump's approach to the Middle East, arguing that the withdrawal from the Iran deal has increased tensions in the region and has made it more difficult to prevent Iran from developing nuclear weapons. Harris has advocated for rejoining the Iran deal and working with international partners to address the country's nuclear program.

Critics of Harris's approach argue that rejoining the Iran deal would embolden the country and would not address the broader issues of Iran's influence in the region and its support for terrorism. They also argue that the Abraham Accords were a significant achievement and that the U.S. should continue to build on them to promote peace and stability in the Middle East.

National Security and Military Policy

Trump's national security policy was characterized by a focus on reducing U.S. involvement in foreign conflicts and bringing American troops home. The administration sought to end the wars in Afghanistan and Iraq and to reduce the U.S. military presence in Syria. Trump argued that the U.S. should not be the world's policeman and that it was time for other countries to take more responsibility for their own security.

The administration also increased defense spending and focused on modernizing the U.S. military, including the creation of the Space Force as a new branch of the armed forces. Supporters of Trump's approach argue that it was necessary to rebuild the military after years of underinvestment and to ensure that the U.S. remains prepared to face new and emerging threats.

Kamala Harris has been critical of Trump's approach to national security, arguing that the U.S. should play a more active role in global security and that reducing the country's involvement in foreign conflicts could create a vacuum that would be filled by adversaries such as Russia and China. Harris has also advocated for re-engaging with international institutions and rebuilding alliances that she argues have been weakened under Trump's leadership.

Critics of Harris's approach argue that a more active role in global security could lead to the U.S. becoming embroiled in new conflicts and that the country should focus on protecting its own interests rather than trying to police the world. They also argue that the U.S. should continue to invest in its military to ensure that it remains the strongest in the world.

Conclusion: The Case for Trump's Foreign Policy

In conclusion, Trump's foreign policy was characterized by a focus on protecting American interests, reducing U.S. involvement in foreign conflicts, and renegotiating trade deals to benefit American workers. His supporters argue that this approach was necessary to address the challenges posed by countries such as China and Iran and to ensure that the U.S. remains a strong and secure nation.

In contrast, Kamala Harris's foreign policy proposals are seen by critics as likely to lead to increased reliance on international institutions, a more cooperative stance towards adversaries, and a reduced focus on protecting American interests. For those who believe that a strong, assertive foreign policy is essential for national security and global leadership, Trump's approach provides a compelling reason to support his re-election.

The 2024 election will have significant implications for U.S. foreign policy and national security, and the decisions made by the next administration will shape the global landscape for years to come. Trump's foreign policy achievements, including the Abraham Accords and the tough stance on China, are seen by his supporters as evidence that his approach is the right one for the country.

Chapter 19: The MAGA Movement and Its Global Impact

The Make America Great Again (MAGA) movement, led by Donald Trump, has been one of the most influential political movements in recent American history. The movement's core principles include a focus on American nationalism, economic protectionism, and a rejection of globalism. Trump's supporters argue that the MAGA movement represents a return to traditional American values and a focus on putting the interests of the American people first.

The Rise of the MAGA Movement

The MAGA movement emerged during Trump's 2016 presidential campaign, with the slogan "Make America Great Again" resonating with many Americans who felt left behind by globalization and the changing economy. The movement was characterized by a rejection of the political establishment, a focus on American sovereignty, and a belief that the U.S. should prioritize its own interests over those of other countries.

Supporters of the MAGA movement argue that it represents a return to traditional American values, including a strong work ethic, self-reliance, and a belief in the importance of family and community. They also argue that the movement's focus on economic protectionism and reducing immigration is necessary to protect American jobs and industries from unfair competition.

Kamala Harris has been a vocal critic of the MAGA movement, arguing that it represents a divisive and exclusionary vision of America. She has advocated for a more inclusive and diverse approach to American identity, with a focus on addressing issues such as income inequality, racial justice, and climate change.

Critics of Harris's approach argue that her focus on inclusivity and diversity could lead to a dilution of traditional American values and that the U.S. should prioritize its own interests over those of other countries. They also argue that the MAGA movement's focus on economic protectionism and reducing immigration is necessary to protect American workers and industries.

Global Impact of the MAGA Movement

The MAGA movement has had a significant impact on the global political landscape, with similar nationalist and populist movements emerging in other countries. Trump's approach to foreign policy, including his "America First" doctrine, has inspired leaders in other countries to adopt similar policies, with a focus on protecting their own interests and reducing their involvement in international institutions.

Supporters of the MAGA movement argue that this global trend represents a rejection of globalism and a return to a more traditional, nation-state-focused approach to international relations. They also argue that the movement's focus on economic protectionism and reducing immigration is necessary to address the challenges posed by globalization and the changing economy.

Kamala Harris has been critical of the global impact of the MAGA movement, arguing that it represents a dangerous trend towards nationalism and isolationism. She has advocated for a more cooperative and multilateral approach to global challenges, with a focus on addressing issues such as climate change, human rights, and economic inequality.

Critics of Harris's approach argue that her focus on global cooperation could lead to the U.S. being taken advantage of by other countries and that the country should prioritize its own interests over those of the global community. They also argue that the MAGA movement's focus on protecting American workers and industries is necessary to address the challenges posed by globalization and the changing economy.

The Future of the MAGA Movement

The future of the MAGA movement will depend on the outcome of the 2024 election and the direction of the next administration. If Trump is re-elected, the movement is likely to continue to shape American politics and foreign policy, with a focus on protecting American interests and rejecting globalism.

If Kamala Harris is elected, the future of the MAGA movement is less certain. Harris has been a vocal critic of the movement and has advocated for a more inclusive and diverse approach to American identity. Her supporters argue that her election would represent a rejection of the divisive and exclusionary rhetoric of the MAGA movement and a return to a more cooperative and multilateral approach to global challenges.

Critics of Harris's approach argue that her focus on inclusivity and diversity could lead to a dilution of traditional American values and that the U.S. should prioritize its own interests over those of other countries. They also argue that the MAGA movement's focus on economic protectionism and reducing immigration is necessary to protect American workers and industries from unfair competition.

Conclusion: The Case for the MAGA Movement

In conclusion, the MAGA movement represents a return to traditional American values, with a focus on protecting American interests, reducing immigration, and rejecting globalism. Trump's supporters argue that the movement is necessary to address the challenges posed by globalization and the changing economy and to ensure that the U.S. remains a strong and secure nation.

In contrast, Kamala Harris's proposals are seen by critics as likely to lead to a dilution of traditional American values and an increased reliance on international institutions. For those who believe that a strong, nationalist approach is essential for the future of the U.S., the MAGA movement provides a compelling reason to support Trump's re-election.

The 2024 election will have significant implications for the future of the MAGA movement and for the direction of American politics. The decisions made by the next administration will determine whether the movement continues to shape American politics and foreign policy or whether it is replaced by a more inclusive and multilateral approach.

Chapter 20: The Media and Public Perception of Trump

Donald Trump's relationship with the media has been one of the most contentious aspects of his presidency and post-presidency. Throughout his time in office, Trump frequently criticized the media, accusing them of bias, dishonesty, and unfair treatment. His supporters argue that the media has been hostile towards Trump and has consistently misrepresented his policies and achievements.

The "Fake News" Phenomenon

One of the most notable aspects of Trump's relationship with the media has been his frequent use of the term "fake news" to describe coverage that he believes is biased or inaccurate. Trump's use of the term has resonated with his supporters, who argue that the media has been unfairly critical of his administration and has downplayed his achievements.

The "fake news" phenomenon has had a significant impact on public perception of the media, with many Americans becoming increasingly distrustful of mainstream news outlets. Trump's supporters argue that the media has consistently misrepresented his policies and achievements and has focused on negative stories to undermine his presidency.

Kamala Harris has been critical of Trump's attacks on the media, arguing that they represent a dangerous assault on press freedom and democracy. Harris has advocated for a free and independent press and has argued that the media plays a crucial role in holding the government accountable.

Critics of Harris's approach argue that the media has been biased in its coverage of Trump and that the "fake news" phenomenon represents a legitimate concern about the accuracy and fairness of news reporting. They also argue that Trump's criticisms of the media are necessary to push back against what they see as a concerted effort to undermine his presidency.

Media Coverage of Trump's Policies and Achievements

Throughout his presidency, Trump frequently criticized the media for what he saw as biased coverage of his policies and achievements. Supporters of Trump argue that the media has downplayed his successes and has focused on negative stories to paint his administration in a bad light.

For example, Trump's supporters argue that the media has not given enough credit to his administration's economic achievements, such as the low unemployment rate and the stock market's performance before the COVID-19 pandemic. They also argue that the media has been overly critical of Trump's handling of the pandemic and has not given enough credit to the administration's efforts to develop and distribute vaccines.

Kamala Harris has defended the media's coverage of Trump, arguing that the press has a responsibility to hold the government accountable and to report on the negative aspects of his administration. Harris has also criticized Trump's attacks on the media, arguing that they undermine press freedom and democracy.

Critics of Harris's approach argue that the media has been biased in its coverage of Trump and has focused too much on negative stories while downplaying his achievements. They also argue that the media has not given enough credit to Trump's policies and has instead focused on controversies and scandals.

Social Media and Public Perception

Social media has played a significant role in shaping public perception of Trump and his relationship with the media. Trump's use of Twitter to communicate directly with the public has been a defining feature of his presidency, allowing him to bypass traditional media outlets and reach his supporters directly.

Supporters of Trump argue that social media has allowed him to communicate his message without the filter of the mainstream media, which they believe has been biased against him. They also argue that social media has given a voice to ordinary Americans who feel that their views are not represented by the traditional media.

Kamala Harris has been critical of Trump's use of social media, arguing that it has contributed to the spread of misinformation and has undermined trust in democratic institutions. Harris has advocated for stronger regulation of social media platforms to address issues such as misinformation and hate speech.

Critics of Harris's approach argue that social media has played a crucial role in allowing ordinary Americans to have a voice in the political process and that attempts to regulate social media could lead to censorship and the suppression of free speech.

Conclusion: The Case for Trump's Media Strategy

In conclusion, Trump's relationship with the media has been one of the most contentious aspects of his presidency, with his supporters arguing that the media has been biased against him and has consistently misrepresented his policies and achievements. The "fake news" phenomenon has had a significant impact on public perception of the media, with many Americans becoming increasingly distrustful of mainstream news outlets.

Trump's use of social media has allowed him to communicate directly with the public and has given a voice to ordinary Americans who feel that their views are not represented by the traditional media. In contrast, Kamala Harris's proposals for stronger regulation of social media and her defense of the mainstream media are seen by critics as likely to lead to censorship and the suppression of free speech.

For those who believe that the media has been biased against Trump and that social media has played a crucial role in allowing ordinary Americans to have a voice in the political process, Trump's media strategy provides a compelling reason to support his re-election.

The 2024 election will have significant implications for the future of the media and public perception of the presidency, and the decisions made by the next administration will shape the relationship between the media and the government for years to come.

Chapter 21: The Legacy of Donald Trump's Presidency

As the 2024 election approaches, the legacy of Donald Trump's presidency continues to be a topic of significant debate. Trump's supporters argue that his presidency represents a transformative period in American history, with a focus on economic nationalism, a rejection of globalism, and a return to traditional American values. His critics, on the other hand, argue that his presidency has been marked by division, controversy, and an erosion of democratic norms.

Economic Nationalism and the "America First" Doctrine

One of the defining features of Trump's presidency was his focus on economic nationalism and the "America First" doctrine. Trump argued that the U.S. had been taken advantage of by other countries for too long and that it was time to prioritize American workers and industries.

This approach was evident in Trump's trade policies, including the imposition of tariffs on Chinese goods, the renegotiation of NAFTA, and the withdrawal from the Trans-Pacific Partnership. Supporters of Trump's economic policies argue that they were necessary to protect American jobs and industries from unfair competition and to reduce the U.S. trade deficit.

Kamala Harris has been critical of Trump's economic nationalism, arguing that it has alienated U.S. allies and has weakened the country's leadership on the global stage. Harris has advocated for a more cooperative and multilateral approach to trade and economic relations, with a focus on addressing global challenges such as climate change and economic inequality.

Critics of Harris's approach argue that her focus on global cooperation could lead to the U.S. being taken advantage of by other countries and that the country should prioritize its own interests over those of the global community. They also argue that Trump's economic policies were necessary to address the challenges posed by globalization and to protect American workers and industries.

The Supreme Court and Judicial Appointments

Another significant aspect of Trump's legacy is his impact on the judiciary, particularly the Supreme Court. During his presidency, Trump appointed three conservative justices to the Supreme Court, shifting the balance of the court to the right. This has had a significant impact on a range of issues, including abortion rights, gun control, and religious freedom.

Supporters of Trump argue that his judicial appointments represent a return to constitutional principles and a rejection of judicial activism. They also argue that the conservative majority on the Supreme Court will protect individual rights and freedoms and prevent the government from overstepping its bounds.

Kamala Harris has been critical of Trump's judicial appointments, arguing that they represent a threat to reproductive rights, civil rights, and other progressive causes. Harris has advocated for reforms to the judiciary, including expanding the number of justices on the Supreme Court, to counterbalance the conservative majority.

Critics of Harris's approach argue that her proposals for judicial reform could undermine the independence of the judiciary and could lead to a politicization of the court. They also argue that Trump's judicial appointments were necessary to protect individual rights and freedoms and to prevent the government from overstepping its bounds.

Division and Polarization

One of the most significant criticisms of Trump's presidency is the division and polarization that it has created in American society. Trump's rhetoric, particularly on issues such as immigration, race, and gender, has been seen by many as inflammatory and divisive. His supporters argue that Trump was simply speaking the truth and that his rhetoric was necessary to push back against political correctness and the left-wing agenda.

Kamala Harris has been critical of Trump's rhetoric, arguing that it has deepened divisions in American society and has undermined the country's democratic norms. Harris has advocated for a more inclusive and unifying approach to politics, with a focus on bringing Americans together and addressing issues such as racial and economic inequality.

Critics of Harris's approach argue that her focus on inclusivity and diversity could lead to a dilution of traditional American values and that the U.S. should prioritize its own interests over those of other countries. They also argue that Trump's rhetoric was necessary to push back against political correctness and the left-wing agenda.

The Legacy of the Trump Presidency

In conclusion, the legacy of Donald Trump's presidency is likely to be a topic of significant debate for years to come. Supporters of Trump argue that his presidency represents a transformative period in American history, with a focus on economic nationalism, a rejection of globalism, and a return to traditional American values. They also argue that Trump's judicial appointments will have a lasting impact on the country and will protect individual rights and freedoms.

Critics of Trump's presidency argue that it has been marked by division, controversy, and an erosion of democratic norms. They also argue that Trump's economic policies have alienated U.S. allies and have weakened the country's leadership on the global stage.

The 2024 election will have significant implications for the legacy of Trump's presidency, and the decisions made by the next administration will shape how his time in office is remembered. The outcome of the election will determine whether Trump's policies and approach to governance continue to shape American politics or whether the country moves in a different direction.

Chapter 23: The Future of the Republican Party

As the 2024 election approaches, the future of the Republican Party is a topic of significant debate. The party has been transformed by Donald Trump's presidency, with a focus on economic nationalism, a rejection of globalism, and a return to traditional American values. However, the party is also facing significant challenges, including deep divisions between its establishment and populist wings, as well as changing demographics and political attitudes.

The Populist Wing and the MAGA Movement

One of the most significant changes to the Republican Party during Trump's presidency has been the rise of the populist wing and the MAGA movement. This wing of the party is characterized by a focus on economic nationalism, a rejection of globalism, and a skepticism of the political establishment.

Supporters of the populist wing argue that it represents a return to traditional American values and a rejection of the political correctness and left-wing agenda that they believe has taken over the country. They also argue that the populist wing is necessary to address the challenges posed by globalization and the changing economy and to protect American workers and industries from unfair competition.

Kamala Harris has been critical of the populist wing and the MAGA movement, arguing that they represent a dangerous trend towards nationalism and isolationism. Harris has advocated for a more cooperative and multilateral approach to global challenges, with a focus on addressing issues such as climate change, human rights, and economic inequality.

Critics of Harris's approach argue that her focus on global cooperation could lead to the U.S. being taken advantage of by other countries and that the country should prioritize its own interests over those of the global community. They also argue that the populist wing and the MAGA movement are necessary to address the challenges posed by globalization and the changing economy.

The Establishment Wing and Traditional Conservatism

The Republican Party's establishment wing, which represents the more traditional conservative values of the party, has been significantly challenged by the rise of the populist wing and the MAGA movement. This wing of the party is characterized by a focus on limited government, free markets, and a strong national defense.

Supporters of the establishment wing argue that it represents the true principles of conservatism and that the populist wing's focus on economic nationalism and protectionism is a departure from these principles. They also argue that the establishment wing is necessary to maintain the party's appeal to a broader electorate and to address the changing demographics and political attitudes of the country.

Kamala Harris has been critical of the establishment wing, arguing that its focus on limited government and free markets has led to increasing economic inequality and has failed to address the challenges posed by globalization and the changing economy. Harris has advocated for a more progressive approach to economic policy, with a focus on addressing issues such as income inequality and climate change.

Critics of Harris's approach argue that her focus on progressive economic policies could lead to increased government intervention in the economy and could undermine the principles of free markets and limited government. They also argue that the establishment wing of the Republican Party is necessary to maintain the party's appeal to a broader electorate and to address the changing demographics and political attitudes of the country.

The Future of the Republican Party

The future of the Republican Party will depend on the outcome of the 2024 election and the direction of the next administration. If Trump is re-elected, the party is likely to continue to be dominated by the populist wing and the MAGA movement, with a focus on economic nationalism, a rejection of globalism, and a return to traditional American values.

If Kamala Harris is elected, the future of the Republican Party is less certain. Harris has been a vocal critic of the MAGA movement and has advocated for a more inclusive and diverse approach to American identity. Her supporters argue that her election would represent a rejection of the divisive and exclusionary rhetoric of the MAGA movement and a return to a more cooperative and multilateral approach to global challenges.

Critics of Harris's approach argue that her focus on inclusivity and diversity could lead to a dilution of traditional American values and that the U.S. should prioritize its own interests over those of other countries. They also argue that the Republican Party's future will depend on its ability to address the changing demographics and political attitudes of the country and to maintain its appeal to a broader electorate.

Chapter 24: Conclusion - The Case for the Republican Party

In conclusion, the future of the Republican Party is likely to be shaped by the outcome of the 2024 election and the direction of the next administration. The party is facing significant challenges, including deep divisions between its establishment and populist wings, as well as changing demographics and political attitudes.

Supporters of the populist wing and the MAGA movement argue that they represent a return to traditional American values and a rejection of globalism and political correctness. They also argue that the populist wing is necessary to address the challenges posed by globalization and the changing economy and to protect American workers and industries from unfair competition.

Critics of the populist wing and the MAGA movement argue that they represent a dangerous trend towards nationalism and isolationism and that the party should focus on a more cooperative and multilateral approach to global challenges. They also argue that the establishment wing of the Republican Party is necessary to maintain the party's appeal to a broader electorate and to address the changing demographics and political attitudes of the country.

The future of the Republican Party will depend on its ability to navigate these challenges and to maintain its relevance in a changing political landscape. The decisions made by the next administration will determine whether the party continues to be dominated by the populist wing and the MAGA movement or whether it returns to its traditional conservative values.

Don't miss out!

Visit the website below and you can sign up to receive emails whenever Digby R. Kerr publishes a new book. There's no charge and no obligation.

https://books2read.com/r/B-A-BKGHC-EXHYE

BOOKS 2 READ

Connecting independent readers to independent writers.

Did you love *DONLAD TRUMP AND THE MAGA MOVEMENT*? Then you should read *"12 Steps to Success: Real-Life Stories of Manifestation and Transformation"*[1] by Digby R. Kerr!

"12 Steps to Success: Real-Life Stories of Manifestation and Transformation" serves as a powerful and comprehensive guide for anyone looking to unlock their full potential and bring their dreams into reality. This book takes readers on a transformative journey, blending practical techniques with deep spiritual insights to help them harness the power of manifestation. Through a series of thoughtfully designed steps,

---

1. https://books2read.com/u/bQXrMd

2. https://books2read.com/u/bQXrMd

it offers a detailed exploration of the Law of Attraction, providing readers with the tools they need to align their thoughts, emotions, and actions with their highest aspirations. The journey begins by introducing the fundamental concepts of manifestation, emphasizing the importance of intention and awareness in shaping one's reality

Read more at https://www.linkedin.com/in/digbyrkerr/.

Also by Digby R. Kerr

The Ripple Effect

The Ripple Effect: "A Fable About Embracing Change and
Thriving in Uncertainty"

The Ripple Effect: "A Fable About Embracing Change and
Thriving in Uncertainty"

Standalone

The Universal Code: Unlocking the Secrets of Happiness,
Wealth, and Health

Mastering LinkedIn: A Comprehensive Guide to Building
Your Profile, Growing Your Audience, and Leveraging
Business Opportunities

The Universal Code: Unlocking the Secrets of Happiness,
Wealth, and Health

Cross-Border Trade Compliance: Navigating the Global
Marketplace

Report on Trends and Challenges in Logistics Hiring

"12 Steps to Success: Real-Life Stories of Manifestation and
Transformation"

Psychological Warfare: 9/11 as a Tool for Manipulation and Control
DONLAD TRUMP AND THE MAGA MOVEMENT

Watch for more at https://www.linkedin.com/in/digbyrkerr/.

About the Author

About the Author

Digby R. Kerr Founder, President & CEO of Logistics Consulting, Inc.Partnered with & Powered by the R+R Group, Family of Companies

Digby R. Kerr is a distinguished global logistics expert and entrepreneur whose profound journey has been marked by both triumphs and trials. From his early life in Borehamwood, London, to his rise in New York and beyond, Digby's path has been a testament to the transformative power of universal principles and personal resilience.

A lifelong learner and seeker of wisdom, Digby has delved deeply into the mysteries of happiness, wealth, and health, drawing from a wealth of knowledge, personal experiences, and interactions with leading experts in psychology, neuroscience, and spirituality. His insights into universal thought and processes have shaped his approach to life and business, guiding him through challenges and leading him to a life of abundance and fulfillment.

In his book, **"Unlocking the Secrets of Happiness, Wealth, and Health,"** Digby shares the transformative teachings and practical strategies that have profoundly impacted his life. By revealing the principles that have helped him navigate his own journey, he offers readers a roadmap to unlock their own potential and achieve their desires. His story is not just one of success but of deep personal transformation, illustrating how understanding and applying universal principles can lead to extraordinary results.

Connect with Digby R. Kerr LinkedIn: Digby R. KerrEmail: DKNYPublishing@icloud.comWebsite: DKNY Publishing

Discover more about Digby's journey, his groundbreaking work, and how his publishing company supports rising star authors with expert guidance and professional support.

Read more at https://www.linkedin.com/in/digbyrkerr/.